Frances I. Sims Fulton

To and Through Nebraska

Frances I. Sims Fulton

To and Through Nebraska

ISBN/EAN: 9783744759168

Printed in Europe, USA, Canada, Australia, Japan

Cover: Foto ©Andreas Hilbeck / pixelio.de

More available books at **www.hansebooks.com**

TO AND THROUGH

NEBRASKA.

BY

A Pennsylvania Girl.

THIS LITTLE WORK, WHICH CLAIMS NO MERIT BUT TRUTH
IS HUMBLY DEDICATED TO THE MANY DEAR FRIENDS,
WHO BY THEIR KINDNESS MADE THE LONG
JOURNEY AND WORK PLEASANT TO

The Author,

FRANCES I. SIMS FULTON.

LINCOLN, NEB.:
JOURNAL COMPANY, STATE PRINTERS,
1884.

A WORD TO THE READER.

If you wish to read of the going and settling of the Nebraska Mutual Aid Colony, of Bradford, Pa., in Northwestern Neb., their trials and triumphs, and of the Elkhorn, Niobrara, and Keya Paha rivers and valleys, read Chapter I.

Of the country of the winding Elkhorn, Chapter II.

Of the great Platte valley, Chapter III.

Of the beautiful Big Blue and Republican, Chapter IV.

Of Nebraska's history and resources in general, her climate, school and liquor laws, and Capital, Chapter V.

If you wish a car-window view of the Big Kinzua Bridge (highest in the world), and Niagara Falls and Canada, Chapter VI.

And now, a word of explanation, that you may clearly understand *just why* this little book—if such it may be called, came to be written. We do not want it to be thought an emigration scheme, but only what a Pennsylvania girl heard, saw, and thought of Nebraska. And to make it more interesting we will give our experience with all the fun thrown in, for we really thought we had quite an enjoyable time and learned lessons that may be useful for others to know. And simply give everything just as they were, and the true color to all that we touch upon, simply stating facts as we gathered them here and there during a stay of almost three months of going up and down, around and across the state from Dakota to Kansas— 306 miles on the S. C. & P. R. R., 291 on the U. P. R. R., and 289 on the B. & M. R. R., the three roads that traverse the state from east to west. It is truly an unbiased work, so do not chip and shave at what may seem incredible, but, as you read, remember you read ONLY TRUTH.

My brother, C. T. Fulton, was the originator of the colony movement; and he with father, an elder brother, and myself were members. My parents, now past the hale vigor of life, consented to go, providing the location was not chosen too far north, and all the good plans and rules were fully carried out. Father made a tour of the state in 1882, and was much pleased with it, especially central Nebraska. I was anxious to "claim" with the rest that I might have a farm to give to my youngest brother, now too young to enter a claim for himself—claimants must be twenty-one years of age. When he was but twelve years old, I promised that for his abstaining from the use of tobacco and intoxicating drinks in every shape and form, until he was twenty-one years old, I would

A WORD TO THE READER.

present him with a watch and chain. The time of the pledge had not yet expired, but he had faithfully kept his promise thus far, and I knew he would unto the end. He had said: "For a gold watch, sister, I will make it good for life;" but now insisted that he did not deserve anything for doing that which was only right he should do; yet I felt it would well repay me for a life pledge did I give him many times the price of a gold watch. What could be better than to put him in possession of 160 acres of rich farming land that, with industry, would yield him an independent living? With all this in view, I entered with a zeal into the spirit of the movement, and with my brothers was ready to go with the rest. As father had served in the late war, his was to be a soldier's claim, which brother Charles, invested with the power of attorney, could select and enter for him. But our well arranged plans were badly spoiled when the location was chosen so far north, and so far from railroads. My parents thought they could not go there, and we children felt we could not go without them, yet they wrote C. and I to go, see for ourselves, and if we thought best they would be with us. When the time of going came C. was unavoidably detained at home, but thought he would be able to join me in a couple of weeks, and as I had friends among the colonists on whom I could depend for care it was decided that I should go.

When a little girl of eleven summers I aspired to the writing of a "yellow backed novel," after the pattern of Beadle's dime books, and as a matter of course planned my book from what I had read in other like fiction of the same color. But already tired of reading of perfection I never saw, or heard tell of except in story, my heroes and heroines were to be only common, every-day people, with common names and features. The plan, as near as I can remember, was as follows:

A squatter's cabin hid away in a lonely forest in the wild west. The squatter is a sort of out-law, with two daughters, Mary and Jane, good, sensible girls, and each has a lover; not handsome, but brave and true, who with the help of the good dog "Danger," often rescues them from death by preying wolves, bears, panthers, and prowling Indians.

The concluding chapter was to be, "The reclaiming of the father from his wicked ways. A double wedding, and together they all abandon the old home, and the old life, and float down a beautiful river to a better life in a new home.'"

Armed with slate and pencil, and hid away in the summer-house, or locked in the library, I would write away until I came to a crack mid-way down the slate, and there I would always pause to read what I had written, and think what to say next. But I would soon be called to my neglected school books, and then would hastily rub out what I had written, lest others would learn of my secret project; yet the story would be re-written as soon as I could again steal away. But the crack in my slate was a bridge I never crossed with my book.

Ah! what is the work that has not its bridges of difficulties to cross? and how often we stop there and turning back, rub out all we have done?

"Rome was not built in a day," yet I, a child, thought to write a book in a day, when no one was looking. I have since learned that it takes lesson and lessons, read and re-read, and many too that are not learned from books, and then the book will be—only a little pamphlet after all.

THROUGH NEBRASKA.

CHAPTER I.

Going and Settling of the Nebraska Mutual Aid Colony of Bradford, Pa., in Northern Nebraska—A Description of the Country in which they located, which embraces the Elkhorn, Niobrara and Keya Paha Valleys—Their First Summer's Work and Harvest.

True loyalty, as well as true charity, begins at home. Then allow us to begin this with words of love of our own native land,—the state of all that proud Columbia holds within her fair arms the nearest and dearest to us; the land purchased from the dusky but rightful owners, then one vast forest, well filled with game, while the beautiful streams abounded with fish. But this rich hunting ground they gave up in a peaceful treaty with the noble Quaker, William Penn; in after years to become the "Keystone," and one of the richest states of all the Union.

Inexhaustible mineral wealth is stored away among her broad mountain ranges, while her valleys yield riches to the farmer in fields of golden grain. Indeed, the wealth in grain, lumber, coal, iron, and oil that are gathered from her bosom cannot be told—affording her children the best of living; but they

they have grown, multiplied, and gathered in until the old home can no longer hold them all; and some must needs go out from her sheltering arms of law, order, and love, and seek new homes in the "far west," to live much the same life our forefathers lived in the land where William Penn said: "I will found a free colony for all mankind."

Away in the northwestern part of the state, in McKean county, a pleasant country village was platted, a miniature Philadelphia, by Daniel Kingbury, in or about the year 1848. Lying between the east and west branches of the Tunagwant—or Big Cove— Creek, and hid away from the busy world by the rough, rugged hills that surround it, until in 1874, when oil was found in flowing wells among the hills, and in the valleys, and by 1878 the quiet little village of 500 inhabitants was transformed into a perfect beehive of 18,000 busy people, buying and selling oil and oil lands, drilling wells that flowed with wealth, until the owners scarce knew what to do with their money; and, forgetting it is a long lane that has no turning, and a deep sea that has no bottom, lived as though there was no bottom to their wells, in all the luxury the country could afford. And even to the laboring class money came so easily that drillers and pumpers could scarce be told from a member of the Standard Oil Company.

Bradford has been a home to many for only a few years. Yet years pass quickly by in that land of excitement: building snug, temporary homes, with every convenience crowded in, and enjoying the society of a free, social, intelligent people. Bradford is a place where all can be suited. The principal churches are well represented; the theaters and operas well sustained. The truly good go hand in hand; those who live for society and the world can find enough to engross their entire time and attention, while the wicked can find depth enough for the worst of living. We have often thought it no wonder that but few were allowed to carry away wealth from the oil country; for, to obtain the fortune sought, many live a life contrary to their hearts' teachings, and only for worldly gain and pleasure. Bradford is nicely situated in the valley "where the waters meet," and surrounded by a chain or net-work of hills, that are called spurs of the Alleghany mountains, which are yet well wooded by a variety of forest trees, that in autumn show innumerable shades and tinges. From among the trees many oil derricks rear their "crowned heads" seventy-five feet high, which, if not a feature of beauty, is quite an added interest and wealth to the rugged hills. From many of those oil wells a flow of gas is kept constantly burning, which livens the darkest night.

Thus Bradford has been the center of one of the richest oil fields, and like former oil metropolis has produced wealth almost beyond reckoning. Many have came poor, and gone rich. But the majority have lived and spent their money even more lavishingly than it came—so often counting on and spending money that never reached their grasp. But as the tubing and drills began to touch the bottom of this great hidden sea of oil, when flowing wells had to be pumped, and dry holes were reported from territory that had once shown the best production, did they begin to reckon their living, and wonder where all their money had gone. Then new fields were tested, some flashing up with a brilliancy that lured many away, only to soon go out, not leaving bright coals for the deluded ones to hover over; and they again were compelled to seek new fields of labor and living, until now Bradford boasts of but 12,000 inhabitants.

Thus people are gathered and scattered by life in the oil country. And to show how fortunes in oil are made and lost, we quote the great excitement of Nov., 1882, when oil went up, up, and oil exchanges, not only at Bradford, but from New York to Cincinnati, were crowded with the rich and poor, old and young, strong men and weak women, investing their every dollar in the rapidly advancing oil.

Many who had labored hard, and saved close, invested their *all;* dreaming with open eyes of a still advancing price, when they would sell and realize a fortune in a few hours.

Many rose the morning of the 9th, congratulating themselves upon the wealth the day would bring.

What a world of pleasure the anticipation brought.

But as the day advanced, the "bears" began to bear down, and all the tossing of the "bulls of the ring" could not hoist the bears with the standard on top. So from $1.30 per barrel oil fell to $1.10. The bright pictures and happy dreams of the morning were all gone, and with them every penny, and often more than their own were swept.

Men accustomed to oil-exchange life, said it was the hardest day they had ever known there. One remarked, that there were not only pale faces there, but faces that were *green* with despair. This was only one day. Fortunes are made and lost daily, hourly. When the market is "dull," quietness reigns, and oilmen walk with a measured tread. But when it is "up" excitement is more than keeping pace with it.

Tired of this fluctuating life of ups and downs, many determined to at last take Horace Greeley's advice and "go west and grow up with the country," and banded themselves together under the title of "The Nebraska Mutual Aid Colony." First called together by C. T. Fulton, of Bradford Pa., in January, 1883, to which about ten men answered. A colony was talked over, and another meeting appointed, which received so much encouragement by way of interest shown and number in attendance, that Pompelion hall was secured for further meetings. Week after week they met, every day adding new names to the list, until they numbered about fifty. Then came the electing of the officers for the year, and the arranging and adopting of the constitution and by-laws. Allow me to give you a summary of the colony laws. Every name signed must be accompanied by the paying of two dollars as an initiation fee; but soon an assessment was laid of five dollars each, the paying of which entitled one to a charter membership. This money was to defray expenses, and purchase 640 acres of land to be platted into streets and lots, reserving necessary grounds for churches, schools, and public buildings. Each charter member was entitled to two lots—a business and residence lot, and a pro rata share of, and interest in the residue of remaining lots. Every member taking or buying lands was to do so within a radius of ten miles of the town site. "The manufacture and sale of spirituous or malt liquors shall forever be prohibited as a beverage. Also the keeping of gambling houses."

On the 13th of March, when the charter membership numbered seventy-three, a committee of three was sent to look up a location.

The committee returned April 10th; and 125 members gathered to hear their report, and where they had located. When it was known it was in northern Nebraska, instead of in the Platte valley, as was the general wish, and only six miles from the Dakota line, in the new county of Brown, an almost unheard of locality, many were greatly disappointed, and felt they could not go so far north, and so near the Sioux Indian reservation, which lay across the line in southern

Dakota. Indeed, the choosing of the location in this unthought-of part of the state, where nothing but government land is to be had, was a general upsetting of many well laid plans of the majority of the people. But at last, after many meetings, much talking, planning, and voting, transportation was arranged for over the Lake Shore and Michigan Southern, Chicago and Northwestern, and Sioux City and Pacific R. Rs., and the 24th of April appointed for the starting of the first party of colonists.

We wonder, will those of the colony who are scattered over the plains of Nebraska, tell, in talking over the "meeting times" when anticipation showed them their homes in the west, and hopes ran high for a settlement and town all their own, tell how they felt like eager pilgrims getting ready to launch their "Mayflower" to be tossed and landed on a wild waste of prairie, they knew not where?

We need scarce attempt a description of the "getting ready," as only those who have left dear old homes, surrounded by every strong hold kindred, church, school, and our social nature can tie, can realize what it is to tear away from these endearments and follow stern duty, and live the life they knew the first years in their new home would bring them; and, too, people who had known the comforts and luxuries of the easy life, that only those who have lived in the oil country can know, living and enjoying the best their money could bring them, some of whom have followed the oil since its first advent in Venango county, chasing it in a sort of butterfly fashion, flitting from Venango to Crawford, Butler, Clarion, and McKean counties (all of Penna.); making and losing fortune after fortune, until, heart-sick and poorer than when they began, they resolve to spend their labor upon something more substantial, and where they will not be crowded out by Standard or monopoly.

The good-bye parties were given, presents exchanged, packing done, homes broken up, luncheon prepared for a three days' journey, and many sleepless heads were pillowed late Monday night to wake early Tuesday morning to "hurry and get ready." 'Twas a cold, cheerless morning; but it mattered not; no one stopped to remark the weather; it was only the going that was thought or talked of by the departing ones and those left behind.

And thus we gathered with many curious ones who came only to see the exodus, until the depot and all about was crowded. Some laughing and joking, trying to keep up brave hearts, while here and there were companies of dear friends almost lost in the sorrow of the "good-bye" hour. The departing ones, going perhaps to never more return, leaving those behind whom they could scarce hope to again see. The aged father and mother, sisters and brothers, while wives and children were left behind for a season. And oh! the multitude of dear friends formed by long and pleasant associations to say "good bye" to forever, and long letters to promise telling all about the new life in the new home.

One merry party of young folks were the center of attraction for the hilarity they displayed on this solemn occasion, many asking, "Are they as merry as they appear?" while they laughed and chattered away, saying all the funny things they could summon to their tongues' end, and all just to keep back the sobs and tears.

Again and again were the "good byes" said, the "God bless you" repeated many times, and, as the hour-hand pointed to ten, we knew we soon must go. True to time the train rolled up to the depot, to take on its load of human freight to be landed 1,300 miles from home. Another clasping of hands in the last hurried farewell, the good wishes repeated, and we were hustled into the train, that soon started with an ominous whistle westward; sending back a wave of tear-stained handkerchiefs, while we received the same, mingled with cheers from encouraging ones left behind. The very clouds seemed to weep a sad farewell in flakes of pure snow, emblematic of the pure love of true friends, which indeed is heaven-born. Then faster came the snow-flakes, as faster fell the tears until a perfect shower had fallen; beautifying the earth with purity, even as souls are purified by love. We were glad to see the snow as it seemed more befitting the departing hour than bright sunshine. Looking back we saw the leader of the merry party, and whose eyes then sparkled with assumed joyousness, now flooded with tears that coursed down the cheeks yet pale with pent up emotion. Ah! where is the reader of hearts, by the smiles we wear, and the songs we sing? Around and among the hills our train wound and Bradford was quickly lost sight of.

But, eager to make the best of the situation, we dried our tears and busied ourselves storing away luggage and lunch baskets, and arranging everything for comfort sake.

This accomplished, those of us who were strangers began making friends, which was an easy task, for were we not all bound together under one bond whose law was mutual aid? All going to perhaps share the same toil and disadvantages, as well as the same pleasures of the new home?

Then we settled down and had our dinners from our baskets. We heard a number complain of a lump in their throat that would scarcely allow them to swallow a bite, although the baskets were well filled with all the good things a lunch basket can be stored with.

When nearing Jamestown, N. Y., we had a good view of Lake Chautauqua, now placid and calm, but when summer comes will bear on her bosom people from almost everywhere; for it is fast becoming one of the most popular summer resorts. The lake is eighteen miles long and three miles wide. Then down into Pennsylvania, again. As we were nearing

Meadville, we saw the best farming land of all seen during the day. No hills to speak of after leaving Jamestown; perhaps they were what some would call hills, but to us who are used to real up-and-down hills, they lose their significance. The snow-storm followed us to Meadville, where we rested twenty minutes, a number of us employing the time in the childish sport of snow-balling. We thought it rather novel to snow-ball so near the month of buds and blossoms, and supposed it would be the last "ball" of the season, unless one of Dakota's big snow-storms would slide over the line, just a little ways, and give us a taste of Dakota's clime. As we were now "all aboard" from the different points, we went calling among the colonists and found we numbered in all sixty-five men, women, and children, and Pearl Payne the only colony babe.

Each one did their part to wear away the day, and, despite the sad farewells of the morning, really seemed to enjoy the picnic. Smiles and jokes, oranges and and bananas were in plenty, while cigars were passed to the gentlemen, oranges to the ladies, and chewing gum to the children. Even the canaries sang their songs from the cages hung to the racks. Thus our first day passed, and evening found us nearing Cleveland—leaving darkness to hide from our view the beautiful city and Lake Erie. We felt more than the usual solemnity of the twilight hour, when told we were going over the same road that was once strewn with flowers for him whom Columbia bowed her head in prayers and tears, such as she never but once uttered or shed before, and brought to mind lines I then had written :

> Bloom now most beautiful, ye flowers,
>   Your loveliness we'll strew
> From Washington to Cleveland's soil,
>   The funeral cortege through.
> In that loved land that gave him birth
>   We lay him down to rest,
> 'Tis but his mangled form alone,
>   His soul is with the blest.
> Not Cleveland's soil alone is moist
>   With many a falling tear,
> A mist is over all this land
>   For him we loved most dear.
>
> " Nearer, my God, to thee," we sing;
>   In mournful strains and slow,
> While in the tomb we gently lay,
>   Our martyred Garfield low.

Songs sang in the early even-tide were never a lullaby to me, but rather the midnight hoot of the owl, so, while others turn seats, take up cushions and place them crosswise from seat to seat, and cuddled down to wooing sleep, I will busy myself with my pen. And as this may be read by many who never climbed a mountain, as well as those who never trod prairie land, I will attempt a description of the land we leave behind us. But Mr. Clark disturbs me every now and then, getting hungry, and thinking "it's most time to eat," and goes to hush Mr. Fuller to sleep, and while doing so steals away his bright, new coffee pot, in which his wife has prepared a two days' drinking; but Mr. C.'s generosity is making way with it in treating all who will take a sup, until he is now rinsing the grounds.

Thus fun is kept going by a few, chasing sleep away from many who fain would dream of home. "Home!" the word we left behind us, and the word we go to seek; the word that charms the weary wandering ones more than all others, for there are found the sweetest if not the richest comforts of life. And of home I now would write; but my heart and hand almost fail me. (I know I cannot do justice to the grand old mountains and hills, the beautiful valleys) and streams that have known us since childhood's happy days, when we learned to love them with our first loving. Everyone goes, leaving some spot dearer than all others behind. 'Tis not that we do not love our homes in the East, but a hope for a better in a land we may learn to love, that takes us west, and also the same spirit of enterprise and adventure that has peopled all parts of the world.

When the sun rose Wednesday morning it found us in Indiana. We were surprised to see the low land, with here and there a hill of white sand, on which a few scrubby oaks grew. It almost gave me an ague chill to see so much ground covered with water that looked as though it meant to stay. Yet this land held its riches, for the farm houses were large and well built, and the fields were already quite green. But these were quickly lost sight of for a view of Lake Michigan, second in size of the five great lakes, and the only one lying wholly in the U. S. Area, 24,000 square miles; greatest length, 340 miles, and greatest width, 88 miles. The waters seemed to come to greet us, as wave after wave rolled in with foamy crest, only to die out on the sandy shore, along which we bounded. And, well, we could only look and look again, and speed on, with a sigh that we must pass the beautiful waters so quickly by, only to soon tread the busy, thronged streets of Chicago.

The height of the buildings of brick and stone gives the streets a decidedly narrow appearance. A party of sight-seers was piloted around by Mr. Gibson, who spared no pains nor lost an opportunity of showing his party every attention. But our time was so limited that it was but little of Chicago we saw. Can only speak of the great court house, which is built of stone, with granite pillars and trimmings. The Chicago river, of dirty water, crowded with fishing and towing boats, being dressed and rigged by busy sailors, was quite interesting. It made us heart-sick to see the poor women and children, who were anxiously looking for coal and rags, themselves only a mere rag of humanity.

I shook my head and said, "wouldn't like to live here," and was not sorry when we were seated in a clean new coach of the S. C. & P. R. R., and rolled out on the C. & N. W. road. Over the switches, past the dirty flagmen, with their inseparable pipe (wonder if they are the husbands and fathers of the coal and rag pickers?) out on to the broad land of Illinois—rolling prairie, we would call it, with scarcely a stump or stone. Farmers turning up the dark soil, and herds of cattle grazing everywhere in the great fields that were fenced about with board, barb-wire, and neatly trimmed hedge fence, the hedge already showing green.

The farms are larger than our eastern farms, for the houses are so far apart; but here there are no hills to separate neighbors.

Crossed the Mississippi river about four P.M., and when mid-way over was told, " now, we are in Iowa." River rather clear, and about a mile in width. Iowa farmers, too, were busy: some burning off the old grass, which was a novel sight to us.

/ Daylight left us when near Cedar Rapids. How queer! it always gets dark just when we come to some interesting place we wanted so much to see)

Well, all were tired enough for a whole night's rest, and looking more like a delegation from "Blackville"—from the soot and cinder-dirt—than a " party from Bradford," and apparently as happy as darkies at a camp-meeting, we sought our rest early, that we might rise about three o'clock, to see the hills of the coal region of Boone county by moonlight. I pressed my face close to the window, and peered out into the night, so anxious to see a hill once more. Travelers from the East miss the rough, rugged hills of home!

The sun rose when near Denison, Iowa,—as one remarked, "not from behind a hill, but right out of the ground"—ushering in another beautiful day.

At Missouri Valley we were joined by Mr. J. R. Buchanan, who came to see us across the Missouri river, which was done in transfer boats—three coaches taken across at a time. As the first boat was leaving, we stood upon the shore, and looked with surprise at the dull lead-color of the water. We knew the word Missouri signified muddy, and have often read of the unchanging muddy color of the water, yet we never realize what we read as what we see. We searched the sandy shore in vain for a pebble to carry away as a memento of the "Big Muddy," but "nary a one" could we find, so had to be content with a little sand. Was told the water was healthy to drink, but as for looks, we would not use it for mopping our floors with. The river is about three-fourths of a mile in width here. A bridge will soon be completed at this point, the piers of which are now built, and then the boats will be abandoned. When it came our turn to cross, we were all taken on deck, where we had a grand view. Looking north and south on the broad, rolling river, east to the bluffy shores of Iowa we had just left, and west to the level lands of Nebraska, which were greeted with "three rousing huzzahs for the state that was to be the future home of so many of our party." Yet we knew the merry shouts were echoed with sighs from sad hearts within. Some, we knew, felt they entered the state never to return, and know no other home.

To those who had come with their every earthly possession, and who would be almost compelled to stay whether they were pleased or not, it certainly was a moment of much feeling. How different with those of us who carried our return tickets, and had a home to return to! It was not expected that all would be pleased; some would no doubt return more devoted to the old home than before.

We watched the leaden waves roll by, down, on down, just as though they had not helped to bear us on their bosom to—we did not know what. How little the waves knew or cared! and never a song they sang to us; no rocks or pebbles to play upon. Truly, "silently flow the deep waters." Only the plowing through the water of the boat, and the splash of the waves against its side as we floated down and across. How like the world are the waters! We cross over, and the ripple we cause dies out on the shore; the break of the wave is soon healed, and they flow on just as before. But, reader, do we not leave footprints upon the shores that show whence we came, and whither we have gone? And where is the voyager upon life's sea that does not cast wheat and chaff, roses and thorns upon the waves as they cross over? Grant, Father, that it may be more of the wheat than chaff, more of the roses than thorns we cast adrift upon the sea of *our* life; and though they may be tempest tossed, yet in Thy hands they will be gathered, not lost.

When we reached the shore, we were again seated in our coach, and switched on to Nebraska's *terra firma*.

Mr. J. R. Buchanan refers to Beaver county, Pa., as his birth-place, but had left his native state when yet a boy, and had wandered westward, and now resides in Missouri Valley, the general passenger agent of the S. C. & P. R. R. Co., which office we afterward learned he fills with true dignity and a generosity becoming the company he represents. He spoke with tenderness of the good old land of Pennsylvania, and displayed a hearty interest in the people who had just come from there. Indeed, there was much kindness expressed for "the colony going to the Niobrara country" all the way along, and many were the compliments paid. Do not blame us for self praise; we flattered ourselves that we *did* well sustain the old family honors of "The Keystone." While nearing Blair, the singers serenaded Mr. B. with "Ten thousand miles away" and other appropriate songs in which he joined, and then with an earnest "God bless you," left us. Reader, I will have to travel this road again, and then I will tell you all about it. I have no time or chance to write now. The day is calm and bright, and more like a real pic-nic or pleasure excursion than a day of travel to a land of "doubt." When the train stopped any time at a station, a number of us would get off, walk about, and gather half-unfolded cottonwood and boxelder leaves until "all aboard" was sung out, and we were on with the rest—to go calling and visit with our neighbors until the next station was reached. This relieved the monotony of the constant going, and rested us from the jog and jolt of the cars.

One of the doings of the day was the gathering of a button string; mementos from the colony folks, that I might remember each one. I felt I was going only to soon leave them—they to scatter over the plains, and I to return perhaps never to again see Nebraska, and 'twas with a mingling of sadness with all the fun of the gathering, that I received a button from this one, a key or coin from that one, and scribbled down the name in my memorandum. I knew they would speak to me long after we had separated, and tell how the givers looked, or what they said as they gave them to me, thinking, no doubt, it was only child's play.

Mr. Gibson continued with the party, just as obliging as ever, until we reached Fremont, where he turned back to look after more travelers from the East, as he is eastern passenger agent of the S. C. & P. R. R. He received the thanks of all for the kindness and patience he displayed in piloting a party of impatient emigrants through a three days' journey.

Mr. Familton, who joined us at Denison, Iowa, and

was going to help the claim hunters, took pity on our empty looking lunch baskets, and kindly had a number to take dinner at West Point and supper at Neligh with him. It was a real treat to eat a meal from a well spread table again.

❲I must say I was disappointed; I had fancied the prairies would already be in waving grass; instead, they were yet brown and sere with the dead grass of last year excepting where they had been run over with fire, and that I could scarcely tell from plowed ground—it has the same rough appearance, and the soil is so very dark.❳ Yet, the farther west we went, the better all seemed to be pleased. Thus, with song and sight-seeing, the day passed. "Old Sol" hid his smiling face from us when near Clearwater, and what a grand "good night" he bade us! and what beauty he spread out before us, going down like a great ball of fire, setting ablaze every little sheet of water, and windows in houses far away! Indeed, the windows were all we could see of the houses.

We were all wide awake to the lovely scene so new to us. Lizzie saw this, Laura that, and Al, if told to look at the lovely sunset (but who had a better taste for wild game) would invariably exclaim: Oh! the prairie chickens! the ducks! the ducks! and wish for his gun to try his luck. Thus nothing was lost, but everything enjoyed, until we stopped at a small town where a couple of intoxicated men, claiming to be cow-boys, came swaggering through our car to see the party of "tenderfeet," as new arrivals from the East are termed by some, but were soon shown that their company was not congenial and led out of the car. My only defense is in flight and in getting out of the way; so I hid between the seats and held my ears. Oh! dear! why did I come west? I thought; but the train whistle blew and away we flew leaving our tormenters behind, and no one hurt. Thus ended our first battle with the much dreaded cowboys; yet we were assured by others that they were not cow-boys, as they, with all their wildness, would not be guilty of such an act.

About 11 o'clock, Thursday night, we arrived at our last station, Stuart, Holt county. Our coach was switched on a side-track, doors locked, blinds pulled down, and there we slept until the dawning of our first morning in Nebraska. The station agent had been apprised of our coming, and had made comfortable the depot and a baggage car with a good fire; that the men who had been traveling in other coaches and could not find room in the two hotels of the town, could find a comfortable resting place for the night.

We felt refreshed after a night of quiet rest, and the salubrious air of the morning put us in fine spirits, and we flocked from the car like birds out of a cage, and could have flown like freed birds to their nests, some forty miles farther north-west, where the colonists expected to find their nests of homes.

But instead, we quietly walked around the depot, and listened to a lark that sang us a sweet serenade from amid the grass close by; but we had to chase it up with a "shoo," and a flying clod before we could see the songster. Then by way of initiation into the life of the "wild west," a mark was pinned to a telegraph pole; and would you believe it, reader, the spirit of the country had so taken hold of us already that we took right hold of a big revolver, took aim, pulled the trigger, and after the smoke had cleared away, looked—and—well—we missed paper and pole, but hit the prairie beyond; where most of the shots were sown that followed.

A number of citizens of Stuart had gathered about to see the "pack of Irish and German emigrants," expected, while others who knew what kind of people were coming, came with a hearty welcome for us. Foremost among these were Messrs. John and James Skirving, merchants and stockmen, who, with their welcome extended an invitation to a number to breakfast. But before going, several of us stepped upon the scales to note the effect the climate would have upon our avoirdupois. As I wrote down 94 lbs., I thought, "if my weight increases to 100 lbs., I will sure come again and stay." Then we scattered to look around until breakfast was ready. We espied a great red-wheeled something—I didn't know what, but full of curiosity went to see.

A gentleman standing near asked: "Are you ladies of the colony that arrived last night?"

"Yes, sir, and we are wondering what this is."

"Why, that's an ox plow, and turns four furrows at one time."

"Oh! we didn't know but that it was a western sulky."

It was amusing to hear the guesses made as to what the farming implements were we saw along the way, by these new farmers. But we went to breakfast at Mr. John Skirving's wiser than most of them as far as ox-plows were concerned.

What a breakfast! and how we did eat of the bread, ham, eggs, honey, and everything good. Just felt as though we had never been to breakfast before, and ate accordingly. That noted western appetite must have made an attack upon us already, for soon after weighing ourselves to see if the climate had affected a change yet, the weight slipped on to—reader, I promised you I would tell you the truth and the whole truth; but it is rather hard when it comes right down to the point of the pen to write ninety-six. And some of the others that liked honey better than I did, weighed more than two pounds heavier. Now what do you think of a climate like that?

But we must add that we afterwards tested the difference in the scales, and in reality we had only eaten—I mean we had only gained one and a half pound from the salubrious air of the morning. Dinner and supper were the same in place, price, and quality, but not in quantity.

When we went to the car for our luggage, we found Mr. Clark lying there trying to sleep.

"Home-sick?" we asked.

"No, but I'm nigh sick abed; didn't get any sleep last night."

No, he was not homesick, only he fain would sleep and dream of home.

First meeting of the N. M. A. C. was held on a board pile near the depot, to appoint a committee to secure transportation to the location.

The coming of the colony from Pennsylvania had been noised abroad through the papers, and people were coming from every direction to secure a home near them, and the best of the land was fast being claimed by strangers, and the colonists felt anxious to be off on the morrow.

The day was pleasant, and our people spent it in seeing what was to be seen in and about Stuart, rendering a unanimous "pleased" in the evening. Mr. John Skirving kindly gave three comfortable rooms above his store to the use of the colonists, and the ladies and children with the husbands went to housekeeping there Friday evening.

Saturday morning. Pleasant. All is bustle and stir to get the men started to the location, and at last with oxen, horses, mules, and ponies, eight teams in all, attached to wagons and hacks, and loaded with the big tent and provisions, they were off. While the ladies who were disappointed at being left behind; merrily waved each load away.

But it proved quite fortunate that we were left behind, as Saturday was the last of the pleasant days. Sunday was cool, rained some, and that western wind commenced to blow. We wanted to show that we were keepers of the Sabbath by attending services at the one church of the town. But, as the morning was unpleasant, we remained at the colony home and wrote letters to the dear ones of home, telling of our safe arrival. Many were the letters sent post haste from Stuart the following day to anxious ones in the East.

In the afternoon it was pleasant enough for a walk across the prairie, about a quarter of a mile, to the Elkhorn river. When we reached the river I looked round and exclaimed: Why! what town is that? completely turned already and didn't know the town I had just left.

The river has its source about fifteen miles southwest of Stuart, and is only a brook in width here, yet quite deep and very swift. The water is a smoky color, but so clear the fish will not be caught with hook and line, spears and seine are used instead.

Like all the streams we have noticed in Nebraska it is very crooked, yet we do not wonder that the water does not know where to run, there is no "up or down" to this country; it is all just over to us; so the streams cut across here, and wind around there, making angles, loops, and turns, around which the water rushes, boiling and bubbling,—cross I guess because it has so many twists and turns to make; don't know what else would make it flow so swiftly in this level country. But hear what Prof. Aughey says:

"The Elkhorn river is one of the most beautiful streams of the state. It rises west of Holt and Elkhorn counties. Near its source the valley widens to a very great breadth, and the bluffs bordering it are low and often inappreciable. The general direction of the main river approximates to 250 miles. Its direction is southeast. It empties into the Platte in the western part of Sarpy county. For a large part of its course the Elkhorn flows over rock bottom. It has considerable fall, and its steady, large volume of waters will render it a most valuable manufacturing region."

We had not realized that as we went west from the Missouri river we made a constant ascent of several feet to the mile, else we would not have wondered at the rapid flow of the river. The clearness of the water is owing to its being gathered from innumerable lakelets; while the smoky color is from the dead grass that cover its banks and some places its bed.

Then going a little farther on we prospected a sod house, and found it quite a decent affair. Walls three feet thick, and eight feet high; plastered inside with native lime, which makes them smooth and white; roof made of boards, tarred paper, and a covering of sod. The lady of the house tells me the house is warm in winter, and cool in summer. Had a drink of good water from the well which is fifteen feet deep, and walled up with barrels with the ends knocked out.

The common way of drawing water is by a rope, swung over a pulley on a frame several feet high, which brings to the top a zinc bucket the shape and length of a joint of stove pipe, with a wooden bottom. In the bottom is a hole over which a little trap door or valve is fastened with leather hinges. You swing the bucket over a trough, and let it down upon a peg fastened there, that raises the trap door and leaves the the water out. Some use a windlass. It seemed awkward to us at first, but it is a cheap pump, and one must get used to a good many inconveniences in a new country. But we who are used to dipping water from springs, are not able to be a judge of pumps. Am told the water is easily obtained, and generally good; though what is called hard water.

(The country is almost a dead level, without a tree or bush in sight. But when on a perfect level the prairie seems to raise around you, forming a sort of dish with you in the center. Can see the sand hills fifteen miles to the southwest quite distinctly.) Farm houses, mostly sod, dot the surrounding country.

Monday, 30th. Cool, with some rain, high wind, and little sunshine. For the sake of a quiet place where I could write, I sought and found a very pleasant stopping place with the family of Mr. John Skirving, of whom I have before spoken, and who had but lately brought his family from Jefferson City, Iowa.

Tuesday. A very disagreeable day; driving rain, that goes through everything, came down all day. Do wonder how the claim hunters in camp near the Keya Paha river will enjoy this kind of weather, with nothing but their tent for shelter.

Wednesday. About the same as yesterday, cold and wet; would have snowed, but the wind blew the flakes to pieces and it came down a fine rain.

Mrs. S. thinks she will go back to Iowa, and I wonder if it rains at home.

Thursday. And still it rains and blows!

Friday. A better day. Last night the wind blew so hard that I got out of bed and packed my satchel preparatory to being blown farther west, and dressed ready for the trip. The mode of travel was so new to me I scarcely knew what to wear. Everything in readiness, I lay me down and quietly waited the going of the roof, but found myself snug in bed in the morning, and a roof over me. The wind was greatly calmed, and I hastened to view the ruins of the storm of the night, but found nothing had been disturbed, only my slumber. The wind seems to make more noise than our eastern winds of the same force; and eastern people seem to make more noise about the wind than western people do. Don't think that I was frightened; there is nothing like being ready for emergencies! I had heard so much of the storms and winds of the West, that I half expected a ride on the clouds before I returned. The clouds cleared away, and the sun shone out brightly, and soon the wind had the mud so dried that it was pleasant walking. The soil is so mixed with sand that the mud is never more than a couple of inches deep here, and is soon dried. When dry a sandy dust settles over everything, but not a dirty dust. A number of the colony men returned to-day.

Saturday. Pleasant. The most of the men have returned. The majority in good heart and looking well despite the weather and exposure they have been subject to, and have selected claims. But a few are discouraged and think they will look for lands elsewhere.

They found the land first thought of so taken that they had to go still farther northwest—some going as far west as Holt creek, and so scattered that but few of them can be neighbors. This is a disappointment not looked for, they expected to be so located that the same church and school would serve them all.

Emigrant wagons have been going through Stuart in numbers daily, through wind and rain, all going in that direction, to locate near the colony. The section they had selected for a town plot had also been claimed by strangers. Yet, I am told, the colonists might have located more in a body had they gone about their claim-hunting more deliberately. And the storm helped to scatter them. The tent which was purchased with colony funds, and a few individual dollars, proved to be a poor bargain. When first pitched there was a small rent near the top, which the wind soon whipped into a disagreeably large opening. But the wind brought the tent to the ground, and it was rightly mended, and hoisted in a more sheltered spot. But, alas! down came the tent again, and as many as could found shelter in the homes of the old settlers.

Some selected their claims, plowed a few furrows, and laid four poles in the shape of a pen, or made signs of improvement in some way, and then went east to Niobrara City, or west to Long Pine, to a land office and had the papers taken out for their claims. Others, thinking there was no need of such hurried precautions, returned to Stuart to spend the Sabbath, and lost their claims. One party selected a claim, hastened to a land office to secure it, and arrived just in time to see a stranger sign his name to the necessary documents making it his.

Will explain more about claim-taking when I have learned more about it.

Sunday, 6 May. Bright and warm. Would not have known there had been any rain during the past week by the ground, which is nicely dried, and walking pleasant.

A number of us attended Sunday school and preaching in the forenoon, and were well entertained and pleased with the manner in which the Sunday school was conducted, while the organ in the corner made it quite home-like. We were glad to know there were earnest workers even here, where we were told the Sabbath was not observed; and but for our attendance here would have been led to believe it were so. Teams going, and stores open to people who come many miles to do their trading on this day; yet it is done quietly and orderly.

The minister rose and said, with countenance beaming with earnestness: "I thank God there are true christians to be found along this Elkhorn valley, and these strangers who are with us to-day show by their presence they are not strangers to Christ; God's house will always be sought and found by his people." While our hearts were filled with thanksgiving, that the God we love is very God everywhere, and unto him we can look for care and protection at all times.

In the evening we again gathered, and listened to a sermon on temperance, which, we were glad to know, fell upon a temperance people, as far as we knew our brother and sister colonists. After joining in "What a friend we have in Jesus" we went away feeling refreshed from "The fountain that freely flows for all," and walked home under the same stars that made beautiful the night for friends far away. Ah! we had began to measure the distance from home already, and did not dare to think how far we were from its shelter.

But, as the stars are, so is God high over all; and

the story of his love is just the same the wide world over.)

Monday. Pleasant. Colonists making preparation to start to the location to-morrow, with their families. Some who have none but themselves to care for, have started.

Tuesday. Rains. Folks disappointed.

Wednesday. Rains and blows. Discouraging.

Thursday. Blows and rains. *Very* discouraging.

The early settlers say they never knew such a long rain at this season. Guess it is raining everywhere; letters are coming telling of a snow in some places nine and ten inches deep, on the 25th of April; of hard frozen ground, and continuous rains. It is very discouraging for the colony folks to be so detained; but they are thankful they are snug in comfortable quarters, in Stuart, instead of out they scarcely know where. Some have prepared muslin tents to live in until they can build their log or sod houses. They are learning that those who left their families behind until a home was prepared for them, acted wisely. I cannot realize as they do the disappointment they have met with, yet I am greatly in sympathy with them.

With the first letter received from home came this word from father: "I feel that my advanced years will not warrant me in changing homes." Well, that settled the matter of my taking a claim, even though the land proved the best. Yet I am anxious to see and know all, now that I am here, for history's sake, and intend going to the colony grounds with the rest. Brother Charley has written me from Plum Creek, Dawson county, to meet him at Fremont as soon as I can, and he will show me some of the beauties of the Platte valley; but I cannot leave until I have done this part of Nebraska justice. Mr. and Mrs. S. show me every kindness, and in such a way that I am made to feel perfectly at home; in turn I try to assist Mrs. S. with her household duties, and give every care and attention to wee Nellie, who is quite ill. I started on my journey breathing the prayer that God would take me into His own care and keeping, and raise up kind friends to make the way pleasant. I trusted all to Him, and now in answer, am receiving their care and protection as one of their own. Thus the time passes pleasantly, while I eat and sleep with an appetite and soundness I never knew before—though I fancy Mrs. S.'s skill as a cook has a bearing on my appetite, as well as the climate—yet every one experiences an increase of appetite, and also of weight. One of our party whom we had called "the pale man" for want of his right name, had thrown aside his "soft beaver" and adopted a stockman's wide rimmed sombrero, traded his complexion to the winds for a bronze, and gained eight pounds in the eleven days he has been out taking the weather just as it came, and wherever it found him.

Friday. Rain has ceased and it shows signs of clearing off.

It does not take long for ground and grass to dry off enough for a prairie fire, and they have been seen at distances all around Stuart at night, reminding us of the gas-lights on the Bradford hills. The prairies look like new mown hay-fields; but they are not the hay-fields of Pennsylvania; a coarse, woody grass that must be burnt off, to allow the young grass to show itself when it comes in the spring. Have seen some very poor and neglected looking cattle that have lived all winter upon the prairie without shelter. I am told that, not anticipating so long a winter, many disposed of their hay last fall, and now have to drive their cattle out to the "divides,"— hills between rivers—to pasture on the prairie; and this cold wet weather has been very hard on them, many of the weak ones dying. It has been a novel sight, to watch a little girl about ten years old herding sheep near town; handling her pony with a masterly hand, galloping around the herd if they begin to scatter out, and driving them into the corral. I must add that I have also seen some fine looking cattle. I must tell you all the bad with the good.

During all this time, and despite the disagreeable weather, emigrants keep up the line of march through Stuart, all heading for the Niobrara country, traveling in their "prairie schooners," as the great hoop-covered wagon is called, into which, often are packed their every worldly possession, and have room to pile in a large family on top. Sometimes a sheet-iron stove is carried along at the rear of the wagon, which, when needed, they set up inside and put the pipe through a hole in the covering. Those who do not have this convenience carry wood with them and build a fire on the ground to cook by; cooking utensils are generally packnd in a box at the side or front. The coverings of the wagons are of all shades and materials; muslin, ducking, ticking, overall stuff, and oil-cloth. When oil-cloth is not used they are often patched over the top with their oilcloth table covers. The women and children generally do the driving, while the men and boys bring up the rear with horses and cattle of all grades, from poor weak calves that look ready to lay them down and die, to fine, fat animals, that show they have had a good living where they came from.

Many of these people are from Iowa, are intelligent and show a good education. One lady we talked with was from Michigan; had four bright little children with her, the youngest about a year old; had come from Missouri Valley in the wagon; but told us of once before leaving Michigan and trying life in Texas; but not being suited with the country, had returned, as they were now traveling, in only a wagon, spending ten weeks on the way. She was driver and nurse both, while her husband attended to several valuable Texas horses.

Another lady said: "Oh! we are from Mizzurie; been on the way three weeks."

"How can you travel through such weather?"

"Oh! we don't mind it, we have a good ducking cover that keeps out the rain, and when the wind blows very hard we tie the wagon down."

"Never get sick?"

"No."

"Not even a cold?"

"Oh! no, feel better now than when we started."

"How many miles can you go in a day?"

"We average about twenty."

The sun and wind soon tans their faces a reddish brown, but they look healthy, happy, and contented. Thus you see, there is a needed class of people in the West that think no hardship to pick up and thus go whither their fancy may lead them, and to this class in a great measure we owe the opening up of the western country.

Saturday morning. Cloudy and threatened more storm, but cleared off nicely after a few stray flakes of "beautiful snow" had fallen. All getting ready to make a start to the colony location. Hearing that Mr. Lewis, one of the colonists, would start with the rest with a team of oxen, I engaged a passage in his wagon. I wanted to go West as the majority go, and enter into the full meaning and spirit of it all; so, much to the surprise of many, I donned a broad brimmed sombrero, and left Stuart about one o'clock, perched on the spring seat of a double bed wagon, in company with Mrs. Gilman, who came from Bradford last week. Mr. Lewis finds it easier driving, to walk, and is accompanied by Mr. Boggs, who I judge has passed his three score years.

Thinking I might get hungry on the way or have to tent out, Mrs. S. gave me a loaf of bread, some butter, meat, and stewed currants to bring along; but the first thing done was the spilling of the juice off the currants.

Come, reader, go with me on my first ride over the plains of Nebraska behind oxen; of course they do not prance, pace, gallop, or trot; I think they simply walk, but time will tell how fast they can jog along. Sorry we cannot give you the shelter of a "prairie schooner," for the wind does not forget to blow, and it is a little cool.

Mr. L. has already named his matched brindles, "Brock and Broady," and as they were taken from the herd but yesterday, and have not been under the yoke long, they are rather untutored; but Mr. L. is tutoring them with a long lash whip, and I think he will have them pretty well trained by the time we reach the end of our journey.

"Whoa, there Broady! get up! it's after one and dear only knows how far we have got to go. Don't turn 'round so, you'll upset the wagon!" We are going directly north-west. This, that looks like great furrows running parallel with the road, I am told, is the old wagon train road running from Omaha to the Black Hills. It runs directly through Stuart, but I took it to be a narrow potato patch all dug up in deep rows. I see when they get tired of the old ruts, they just drive along side and make a new road which soon wears as deep as the old. No road taxes to pay or work done on the roads here, and never a stone to cause a jolt. The jolting done is caused in going from one rut to another.

Here we are four miles from Stuart, and wading through a two-mile stretch of wet ground, all standing in water. No signs of habitation, not even Stuart to be seen from this point.

Mr. Lewis wishes for a longer whip-stock or handle; I'll keep a look out and perhaps I will find one.

Now about ten miles on our way and Stuart in plain view. There must be a raise and fall in the ground that I cannot notice in going over it. Land is better here Mr. B. says, and all homesteaded. Away to our right are a few little houses, sod and frame. While to the left, 16 miles away, are to be seen the sand-hills, looking like great dark waves.

The walking is so good here that I think I will relieve the—oxen of about 97 pounds. You see I have been gaining in my avoirdupois. I enjoy walking over this old road, gathering dried grasses and pebbles, wishing they could speak and tell of the long emigrant trains that had tented at night by the wayside; of travelers going west to find new homes away out on the wild plains; of the heavy freight trains carrying supplies to the Indian agencies and the Black Hills; of the buffalo stampede and Indian "whoop" these prairies had echoed with, but which gave way to civilization only a few years ago, and now under its protection, we go over the same road in perfect safety, where robbery and massacres have no doubt been committed. Oh! the change of time!

Twelve miles from Stuart, why would you believe it, here's a real little hill with a small stream at the bottom. Ash creek it is called, but I skip it with ease, and as I stop to play a moment in the clear water and gather a pebble from its gravelly bed, I answer J. G. Holland in Kathrina with: Surely, "the crystal brooks *are* sweeter for singing to the thirsty brutes that dip their bearded muzzles in their foam," and thought what a source of delight this little stream is to the many that pass this way. Then viewed the remains of a sod house on the hillside, and wondered what king or queen of the prairie had reigned within this castle of the West, the roof now tumbled in and the walls falling.

Ah! there is plenty of food for thought, and plenty of time to think as the oxen jog along, and I bring up the rear, seeing and hearing for your sake, reader.

Only a little way from the creek, and we pass the first house that stands near the road, and that has not been here long, for it is quite new. The whitehaired children playing about the door will not bother their neighbors much, or get out of the yard and run off for awhile at least, as there is no other house in sight, and the boundless prairie is their dooryard. Happy mother! Happy children!

Now we are all aboard the wagon, and I have read what I have written of the leave taking of home; Mr. B. wipes his eyes as it brings back memories of the good byes to him; Mr. L. says, "that's very truly written," and Mrs. G. whispers, "I must have one of your books, Sims." All this is encouraging, and helps me to keep up brave heart, and put forth every effort to the work I have begun, and which is so much of an undertaking for me.

"Oh! Mr. Lewis, there it is!"

"Is what?"

"Why, that stick for a whip-handle."

I had been watching all the way along, and it was the only stick I had seen, and some poor unfortunate had lost it.

The sun is getting low, and Mr. L. thinks we had better stop over night at this old log-house, eighteen miles from Stuart, and goes to talk to the landlord about lodging. I view the prospects without and think of way-side inns I have read of in story, but never seen before, and am not sorry when he returns and reports: "already crowded with travelers," and flourishing his new whip starts Brock and Broady, though tired and panting, into a trot toward the Niobrara, and soon we are nearing another little stream called Willow creek, named from the few little willow bushes growing along its banks, the first bushes seen all the way along. It is some wider than Ash creek, and as there is no bridge we must ride across. Mr. L. is afraid the oxen are thirsty and will go straight for the water and upset the wagon. Oh, dear! I'll just shut my eyes until we are on the other side.

There, Mr. B. thinks he sees a nest of prairie chicken eggs and goes to secure some for a novelty, but changes his mind and thinks he'll not disturb that nest of white puff-balls, and returns to the wagon quite crestfallen. Heavy looking clouds gathering in the west, obscure the setting sun, which is a real disappointment. The dawning and fading of the days in Nebraska are indeed grand, and I did so want a sunset feast this evening, for I could view it over the bluffy shores of the Niobrara river. Getting dark again, just when the country is growing most interesting.

Mr. B. and L. say, "bad day to-morrow, more rain sure;" I consult my barometer and it indicates fair weather. If it is correct I will name it Vennor, if not I shall dub it Wiggins. Thermometer stands at 48°, think I had better walk and get warmed up; a heavy cloth suit, mohair ulster and gossamer is scarcely sufficient to keep the chilly wind out.

One mile further on and darkness overtakes us while sticking on the banks of Rock creek, a stream some larger than Willow creek, and bridged with poles for pedestrians, on which we crossed; but the oxen, almost tired out, seemed unequal for the pull up the hill. Mr. L. uses the whip, while Mr. B. pushes, and Mrs. G. and I stand on a little rock that juts out of the hill—first stone or rock seen since we entered the state, and pity the oxen, but there they stick. Ah! here is a man coming with an empty wagon and two horses; now he will help us up the hill. "Can you give me a lift?" Mr. L. asks. "I'm sorry I can't help you gentlemen, but that off-horse is *terribly weak*. The other horse is all right, but you can see for yourself, gentlemen, how weak that off-horse is." And away he goes, rather brisk for a weak horse. While we come to the conclusion that he has not been west long enough to learn the ways of true western kindness. (We afterwards learned he was lately from Pennsylvania.) But here comes Mr. Ross and Mr. Connelly who have walked all the way from Stuart. Again the oxen pull, the men push, but not a foot gained; wagon only settling firmer into the mud. The men debate and wonder what to do. "Why not unload the trunks and carry them up the hill?" I ask. Spoopendike like, some-one laughed at my suggestion, but no sooner said than Mr. L. was handing down a trunk with, "That's it—only thing we can do; here help with this trunk," and a goodly part of the load is carried to the top of the hill by the men, while I carry the guns. How brave we are growing, and how determined to go west; and the oxen follow without further trouble.

When within a mile and a half of the river, those of us who can, walk, as it is dangerous driving after dark, and we take across, down a hill, across a little canyon, at the head of which stands a little house with a light in the window that looks inviting, but on we go, across a narrow channel of the river, on to an island covered with diamond willow bushes, and a few trees. See a light from several "prairie schooners" that have cast anchor amid the bushes, and which make a very good harbor for these ships of the west.

"What kind of a shanty is this?"

"Why that is a wholesale and retail store, but the merchant doesn't think worth while to light up in the evening."

On we walk over a sort of corduroy road made of bushes, and so tired I can scarcely take another step.

"Well, is this the place?" I asked as we stopped to look in at the open door of a double log house, on a company of people who are gathered about an organ and singing, "What a friend we have in Jesus."

"No, just across the river where you see that light."

Another bridge is crossed, and we set us down in Aunty Slack's hotel about 9 o'clock. Tired? yes, and *so glad* to get to *somewhere*.

Mr. John Newell, who lives near the Keya Paha, left Stuart shortly after we did, with Mrs. and Miss Lizzie, Laura, and Verdie Ross, in his hack, but soon passed us with his broncho ponies and had reached here before dark.

Three other travelers were here for the night, a Keya Paha man, a Mr. Philips, of Iowa, and Mr. Truesdale, of Bradford, Pa.

"How did the rest get started?" Mrs. R. asks of her husband.

"Well, Mr. Morrison started with his oxen, with Willie Taylor, and Mrs. M. and Mrs. Taylor rode in the buggy tied to the rear end of the wagon. Mr. Barnwell and several others made a start with his team of oxen. But Mr. Taylor's horses would not pull a pound, so he will have to take them back to the owner and hunt up a team of oxen." We had expected to all start at the same time, and perhaps tent out at night. A good supper is refreshing to tired travelers, but it is late before we get laid down to sleep. At last the ladies are given two beds in a new apartment just erected last week, and built of cedar logs with a sod roof, while the men throw themselves down on blankets and comforts on the floor, while the family occupies the old part.

About twelve o'clock the rain began to patter on the sod shingles of the roof over head, which by dawn was thoroughly soaked, and gently pouring down upon the sleepers on the floor, causing a general uprising, and driving them from the room. It won't leak on our side of the house, so let's sleep awhile longer; but just as we were dropping into the arms of Morpheus, spat! came a drop on our pillow, which said, "get up!" in stronger terms than mother ever did. I never saw a finer shower inside a house before. What a crowd we made for the little log house, 14x16 feet, built four years ago, and which served as kitchen, dining room, chamber, and parlor, and well crowded with furniture, without the addition of fourteen rain-bound travelers, beside the family, which consisted of Mrs. Slack, proprietress, a daughter and son-in-law, and a hired girl, 18 heads in all to be sheltered by this old sod roof made by a heavy ridge pole, or log laid across at the comb, which supports slabs or boards laid from the wall, then brush and dried grass, and then the sod. The walls are well chinked and whitened. The door is the full height of the wall, and the tallest of the men have to strictly observe etiquette, and bow as they enter and leave the house. Mr. Boggs invariably strikes a horse shoe suspended to the ceiling with his head, and keeps "good luck" constantly on the swing over us. The roof being old and well settled, keeps it from leaking badly; but Mrs. S. says there is danger of it sliding off or caving in. Dear me! I feel like crawling under the table for protection.

Rain! rain! think I will give the barometer the full name of R. Stone Wiggins! Have a mind to throw him into the river by way of immersion, but fear he would stick in a sand-bar and never predict another storm, so will just hang him on the wall out side to be sprinkled.

The new house is entirely abandoned, fires drowned

out, organ, sewing machine, lunch baskets, and bedding protected as well as can be with carpet and rubber coats.

How glad I am that I have no luggage along to get soaked. My butter and meat was lost out on the prairie or in the river—hope it is meat cast adrift for some hungry traveler—and some one has used my loaf for a cushion, and how sad its countenance! Don't care if it does get wet! So I just pin my straw hat to the wall and allow it to rain on, as free from care as any one can be under such circumstances. I wanted experience, and am being gratified, only in a rather dampening way. Some find seats on the bed, boxes, chairs, trunk, and wood-box, while the rest stand. We pass the day talking of homes left behind and prospects of the new. Seven other travelers came in for dinner, and went again to their wagons tucked around in the canyons.

The house across the river is also crowded, and leaking worse than the *hotel* where we are stopping. Indeed, we feel thankful for the shelter we have as we think of the travelers unprotected in only their wagons, and wonder where the rest of our party are.

The river is swollen into a fretful stream and the sound of the waters makes us even more homesick.

"More rain, more grass," "more rain, more rest," we repeated, and every thing else that had a jingle of comfort in it; but oftener heard, " I *do wish* it would stop!" "When *will* it clear off?" " Does it *always* rain here?" It did promise to clear off a couple of times, only to cloud up again, and so the day went as it came, leaving sixteen souls crowded in the cabin to spend the night as best we could. Just how was a real puzzle to all. But midnight solves the question. Reader, I wish you were here, seated on this spring wagon seat with me by the stove, I then would be spared the pain of a description. Did you ever read Mark Twain's "Roughing It?" or "Innocents Abroad?" well, there are a few *innocents abroad*, just now, *rouyhing it* to their hearts' content.

The landlady, daughter, and maid, with Laura, have laid them down crosswise on the bed. The daughter's husband finds sleep among some blankets, on the floor at the side of the bed. Mr. Ross, almost sick, sticks his head under the table and feet under the cupboard and snores. Mrs. Ross occupies the only rocker—there, I knew she would rock on Mr. Philips who is stretched out on a *one* blanket just behind her! Double up, Mr. P., and stick your knees between the rockers and you'll stand a better chance.

If you was a real birdie, Mrs. Gilman, or even a chicken, you might perch on the side of that box. To sleep in that position would be dangerous; dream of falling sure and might not be all a dream, and then, Mr. Boggs would be startled from his slumbers. Poor man! We do pity him! Six feet two inches tall; too much to get all of himself fixed in a comfortable position at one time. Now bolt upright on a chair, now stretched out on the floor, now doubled up; and now he is on two chairs looking like the last grasshopper of the raid. Hush! Lizzie, you'll disturb the thirteen sleepers.

Mr. Lewis has turned the soft side of a chair up for a pillow before the stove, and list—he snores a dreamy snore of home-sweet-ho-om-me.

Mr. Truesdal is rather fidgety, snugly tucked in behind the stove on a pile of kindling wood. I'm afraid he will black his ears on the pots and kettles that serve as a back ground for his head, but better that than nothing. Am afraid Mr. Newell, who is seated on an inverted wooden pail, will loose his head in the wood-box, for want of a head rest, if he doesn't stop nodding so far back.

Hold tight to your book, Mr. N., you may wake again and read a few more words of Kathrina.

Here, Laura, get up and let your little sister, Verdie, lie down on the bed. "That table is better to eat off than sleep on," Lizzie says, and crawls down to claim a part of my wagon seat in which I have been driving my thoughts along with pencil and paper, and by way of a jog, give the stove a punch with a stick of wood, every now and then; casting a sly glance to see if the old lady looks cross in her sleep, because we are burning all her dry wood up, and dry wood is a rather scarce article just now. But can't be helped. The feathery side of these boards are down, the covers all wet in the other room, and these sleepers must be kept warm.

· Roll over, Mr. Lewis, and give Mrs. Ross room whereon to place her feet and take a little sleep! Now Mrs. R.'s feet are not large if she does weigh over two hundred pounds; small a plenty ; but not quite as small as the unoccupied space, that's all.

Well, it's Monday now, 'tis one o'clock, dear me; wonder what ails my eyes; feels like there's sand in them. I wink, and wink, but the oftener, the longer. Do believe I'm getting sleepy too! What *will* I do? To sleep here would insure a nod over on the stove; no room on the floor without danger of kicks from booted sleepers. Lizzie, says, "Get up on the table, Sims," it will hold a little thing like you. So I leave the seat solely to her and mount the table, fully realizing that "necessity is the mother of invention," and that western people do just as they can, mostly. So

>All cuddled up together,
>In a little weenty heap,
>I double up my pillow
>And laugh myself to sleep.
>I know you will not blame me
>If I dream of home so bright—
>I'll see you in the morning
>So now a kind " good night "

As there is no room for the muses to visit me here I'll not attempt further poetizing but go to sleep and dream I am snug in my own little bed at home. Glad father and mother do not know where their daughter is seeking rest for to-night.

"Get up, Sims, it's five o'clock and Mrs. S. wants to set the table for breakfast," and I start up, rubbing my eyes, wishing I could sleep longer, and wondering why I hadn't come west long ago, and hadn't always slept on a table?

I only woke once during the night, and as the lamp was left burning, could see that Mrs. R. had found a place for her feet, and all were sound asleep. Empty stomachs, weariness, and dampened spirits are surely three good opiates which, taken together, will make one sleep in almost any position. Do wonder if "Mark" ever slept on an extension table when he was out west? Don't think he did, believe he'd use the dirty floor before he'd think of the table; so I am ahead in this chapter.

Well, the fun was equal to the occasion, and I think no one will ever regret the time spent in the little log house at "Morrison's bridge," and cheerfully paid their $1.75 for their four meals and two nights' lodging, only as we jogged along through the cold next day, all thought they would have had a bite of supper, and not gone hungry to the floor, to sleep.

Monday morning. Cold, cloudy, and threatening more rain. Start about eight o'clock for the Keya Paha, Mr. N. with the Ross ladies ahead, while the walkers stay with our "span of brindles" to help push them up the hill, and I walk to relieve them of my weight.

But we have reached the table-land, and as I have made my impress in the sand and mud of this hill of science, I gladly resume my seat in the wagon with Mrs. Gilman, who is freezing with a blanket pinned on over her shawl. Boo! The wind blows cold, and it sprinkles and tries to snow, and soon I too am almost freezing with all my wraps on, my head well protected with fascinator, hat, and veil. How foolish I was to start on such a trip without good warm mittens. "Let's get back on the trunks, Mrs. G., and turn our backs to the wind." But that is not all sufficient and Mr. L. says he cannot wear his overcoat while walking and kindly offers it to me, and I right willingly crawl into it, and pull it up over my ears, and draw my hands up in the sleeves, and try hard to think I am warm. I can scarcely see out through all this bundling, but I must keep watch and see all I can of the country as I pass along. Yet, it is just the same all the way, with the only variation of, from level, to slightly undulating prairie land. Not a tree, bush, stump, or stone to be seen. Followed the old train road for several miles and then left it, and traveled north over an almost trackless prairie. During the day's travel we met but two parties, both of whom were colonists on their way to Long Pine to take claims in that neighborhood. Passed close to two log houses just being built, and two squads of tenters who peered out at us with their sunburnt faces looking as contented as though they were perfectly satisfied with their situation.

The oxen walked right along, although the load was heavy and the ground soft, and we kept up a steady line of march toward the Keya Paha, near where most of the colonists had selected their claims, and as we neared their lands, the country took on a better appearance.

The wind sweeps straight across, and the misting rain from clouds that look to be resting upon the earth, makes it a very gloomy outlook, and very disagreeable. Yet I would not acknowledge it. I was determined, if possible, to make the trip without taking cold. So Mrs. G. and I kept up the fun until we were too cold to laugh, and then began to ask: "How much farther do we have to go? When will we reach there?" Until we were ashamed to ask again, so sat quiet, wedged down between trunks and a plow, and asked no more questions.

"Oh, joy! Mrs. G., there's a house; and I do believe that is Mrs. Ross with Lizzie and Laura standing at the door. I'll just wave them a signal of distress, and they will be ready to receive us with open arms."

And soon we are safely landed at Mr. J. Newell's door, where a married brother lives. They gave us a kindly welcome, and a good warm dinner. After we had rested, Mr. N. took the ladies three miles farther on to the banks of the Keya Paha river, which is 18 miles from the Niobrara and 48 from Stuart, arriving there about four P.M.

Mr. and Mrs. John Kuhn, with whom the party expected to make their home until they could get their tents up, received us very kindly, making us feel quite at home.

Mrs. K. is postmistress of Brewer postoffice, and her table was well supplied with good reading matter. I took up a copy of "Our Continent" to read while I rested, and opened directly to a poem by H. A. Lavely:

> "The sweetest songs are never sung;
> The fairest pictures never hung;
> The fondest hopes are never told—
> They are the heart's most cherished gold."

They were like a voice directly from the pleasant days of last summer, when the author with his family was breathing mountain air at DuBois City, Pa., when we exchanged poems of our own versing, and Mrs L. added her beautiful children's stories.

He had sent them to me last Christmas time, just after composing them, and now I find them in print away on the very frontier of civilization. How little writers know how far the words they pen for the public to read, will reach out! Were they prophetic for our colonists?

Tuesday, 15th of May, dawned without a cloud, and how bright everything looks when the clouds have rolled away. Why, the poor backward buds look as though they would smile right open. What a change from that of yesterday! Reader, I wish I could tell you all about my May day, but the story is a long one—too long for the pages of my little book.

And now Mrs. Ross and the girls are ready with baskets to go with me to gather what we can find in the way of flowers and leaves along the hillside and valley of the Keya Paha. For flowers we gather blossoms of the wild plum, cherry, and currant, a flower they call buffalo beans, and one little violet. But the leaves were not forgotten, and twigs were gathered of every different tree and bush then in leaf. They were of the box elder, wild gooseberry, and buck bush or snow berry. Visited the spring where Mr. Kuhn's family obtained their water; a beautiful place, with moss and overhanging trees and bushes, and altogether quite homelike. Then to the river where we gathered pebbles of almost every color from the sandy shore. We threw, and threw, to cast a stone on the Dakota side, and when this childish play was crowned with success, after we had made many a splash in the water, we returned to the house where Mr. J. Newell waited for us with a spring wagon, and in which, Lizzie, Laura and I took seats, and were off to visit the Stone Butte, twelve miles west.

Up on the table-land we drove, then down into the valley; and now close to the river, and now up and down over the spurrs of the bluff; past the colonists' tent, and now Mr. N. has invited a Miss Sibolt and Miss Minn to join our maying party.

The bottom land shows a luxuriant growth of grass of last year's growing, and acres of wild plum and choke cherry bushes, now white with blossoms, and so mingled that I cannot tell them apart. If they bear as they blossom, there will be an abundance of both. A few scattered trees, mostly burr or scrub oak and elms are left standing in the valley; but not a tree on the table-land over which the road ran most of the way. The Stone Butte is an abrupt hill, or mound, which stands alone on a slightly undulating prairie. It covers a space of about 20 acres at the base; is 300 feet from base to the broad top; it is covered with white stones that at a distance give it the appearance of a snow capped mountain, and can be seen for many miles. Some say they are a limestone, and when burnt, make a good quality of lime; others that they are only a sand-stone. They leave a chalky mark with the touch, and to me are a curious formation, and look as though they had been boiled up and stirred over from some great mush pot, and fell in a shower of confusion just here, as there are no others to be seen but those on the butte. Oh! what a story they could tell to geologists; tell of ages past when these strange features of this wonderful country were formed! But they are all silent to me, and I can only look and wonder, and turn over and look under for some poor Indian's hidden treasure, but all we found were pieces of petrified wood and bone, a moss agate, and a little Indian dart. Lizzie found a species of dandelion, the only flower found on the butte, and gave it to me, for I felt quite lost without a dear old dandelion in my hand on my May day, and which never failed me before. I have termed them "Earth's Stars," for they will peep through the grassy sod whenever the clouds will allow. It is the same in color, but single, and the leaves different.

We called and hallooed, an echo coming back to us from, we did not know where; surely not from Raymond's buttes, which we can see quite distinctly, though they are thirty-five miles away. Maybe 'twas a war whoop from a Sioux brave hid among the bluffs, almost four miles to the north, and we took it for an echo to our own voice. The view obtained from this elevated point was grand.

A wide stretch of rolling prairie, with the Keya Paha river to the north. Though the river is but two and one-half miles away, yet the water is lost to view, and we look beyond to the great range of bluffs extending far east and west along its northern banks, and which belong to the Sioux Indian reservation, they are covered with grass, but without shrubbery of any kind, yet on their sides a few gray stones or rocks can be seen even from here. South of the butte a short distance is a small stream called Holt Creek. Near it we can see two "claim takers" preparing their homes; aside from these but two other houses, a plowman, and some cattle are the only signs of life. Mr. N. tells me the butte is on the claim taken by Mr. Tiffiny, and Messrs. Fuller's and Wood's and others of the colony are near. After all the sight-seeing and gathering is done, I sit me down on a rock all alone, to have a quiet think all to myself. Do you wonder, reader, that I feel lonely and homesick, amid scenes so strange and new? Wonder will our many friends of the years agone think of me and keep the day for me in places where, with them, I have gathered the wild flowers and leaves of spring?

But Mr. N. comes up and interrupts me with: "Do you know, Miss Fulton, your keeping a May-day seems so strange to me? Do not think our western girls would think of such a thing!"

"Since you wonder at it, I will tell you, very briefly, my story. It was instituted by mere accident by me in 1871, and I have kept the 15th of May of every year since then in nature's untrained gardens, gathering of all the different flowers and leaves that are in bloom, or have unfolded, and note the difference in the seasons, and also the difference in the years to me.

No happier girl ever sang a song than did I on my first May-day; and the woodland was never more beautiful, dressed in the bright robes of an early spring. Every tree in full leaf, every wild flower of spring in bloom, and I could not but gather of all—even the tiniest.

The next 15th of May, I, by mere happening,

went to the woods, and remembering it was the anniversary of my accidental maying of the previous year, I stopped to gather as before; but the flowers were not so beautiful, nor the leaves so large. Then, too, I was very sad over the serious illness of a loved sister.

I cannot tell of all the years, but in '74 I searched for May flowers with tear-dimmed eyes—sister May was dead, and everywhere it was desolate.

'75. "A belated snow cloud shook to the ground" a few flakes, and we gathered only sticks for bouquets, with buds scarcely swollen.

In '81, I climbed Point McCoy near Bellefont, Pa., a peak of the Muncy mountains and a range of the Alleghanys, and looked for miles, and miles away, over mountains and vales, and gathered of flowers that almost painted the mountain side, they were so plentiful and bright.

Last year I gathered the flowers of home with my own dear mother, and shared them with May, by laying them on her grave.

To-day, all things have been entirely new and strange; but while I celebrate it on the wild boundless plains of Nebraska, yet almost untouched by the hand of man, dear father and mother are visiting the favorite mossy log, the spring in the wood, and the moss covered rocks where we children played at "house-keeping," and in my name, will gather and put to press leaves and flowers for me. Ah! yes! and are so lonely thinking of their daughter so far away.

The sweetest flower gathered in all the years was Myrtle—sister Maggie's oldest child—who came to me for a May-flower in '76.

But while the flowers bloomed for my gathering in '81, the grass was growing green upon her grave. And I know sister will not forget to gather and place on the sacred mound, "Auntie Pet's" tribute of love.

Thus it is with a mingling of pleasures and pains, of smiles and tears that I am queen of my maying, with no brighter eyes to usurp my crown, for it is all my own day and of all the days of the year the dearest to me.

"I think, Mr. Newell, we can live *good* lives and yet not make the *most* of life; our lives need crowding with much that is good and useful; and this is only the crowding in of a day that is very good and useful to me. For on this day I retrospect the past, and think of the hopes that bloomed and faded with the flowers of other years, and prospect the future, and wonder what will the harvest be that is now budding with the leaves for me and which I alone must garner."

After a last look at the wide, wide country, that in a few years will be fully occupied with the busy children of earth, we left "Stone Butte," carrying from its stony, grassy sides and top many curious mementos of our May-day in Nebraska.

Then I went farther north-west to visit the home

of a "squaw man"—the term used for Indians who cannot endure the torture of the sun dance, and also white men that marry Indian maidens. On our way we passed a neatly built sod house, in which two young men lived who had lately come from Delaware, and were engaged in stock-raising, and enjoyed the life because they were doing well, as one of them remarked to Mr. N. I tell these little things that those who do not already know, may understand how Nebraska is populated with people from everywhere.

Soon we halted at the noble (?) white man's door, and all but Lizzie ventured in, and by way of excuse asked for a drink or *minnie* in the Sioux language. "Mr. Squaw" was not at home, and "Mrs. Squaw," poor woman, acted as though she would like to hide from us, but without a word handed us a dipper of water from which we very lightly sipped, and then turned her back to us, and gave her entire attention to a bright, pretty babe which she held closely in her arms, and wrapped about it a new shawl which hung about her own shoulders. The children were bright and pretty, with brown, curly hair, and no one would guess there was a drop of Indian blood in their veins. But the mother is only a half-breed, as her father was a Frenchman. Yet in features, at least, the Indian largely predominates. Large powerful frame, dusky complexion, thin straight hair neatly braided into two jet black braids, while the indispensable brass ear drops dangled from her ears. Her dress was a calico wrapper of no mean color or make-up. We could not learn much of the expression of her countenance, as she kept her face turned from us, and we did not wish to be rude. But standing thus she gave us a good opportunity to take a survey of their *tepee*. The house was of sod with mother earth floors, and was divided into two apartments by calico curtains. The first was the kitchen with stove, table, benches, and shelves for a cupboard. The room contained a bed covered with blankets, which with a bench was all that was to be seen except the walls, and they looked like a sort of harness shop. The furniture was all of home make, but there was an air of order and neatness I had not expected.

The woman had been preparing kinnikinic tobacco for her white chief to smoke. It is made by scraping the bark from the red willowg, then drying, and usually mixing with an equal quantity of natural leaf tobacco, and is said to make "pleasant smoking." Ah, well! I thought, it is only squaws that will go to so much pains to supply their liege lords with tobacco. She can, but will not speak English, as her husband laughs at her awkward attempts. So not a word could we draw from her. She answered our "good bye," with a nod of the head and a motion of the lips. I know she was glad when the "pale faces" were gone, and we left feeling so sorry for her and indignant, all agreeing that any man who would marry a squaw is not worthy of even a squaw's love and labor; labor is what they expect and demand of them, and as a rule, the squaw is the better of the two. Their husbands are held in great favor by those of their own tribe, and they generally occupy the land allowed by the government to every Indian, male or female, but which the Indians are slow to avail themselves of. They receive blankets and clothing every spring and fall, meat every ten days, rations of sugar, rice, coffee, tobacco, bread and flour every week.

Indians are not considered as citizens of the United States, and have no part in our law-making, yet are controlled by them. They are kept as Uncle Sam's unruly subjects, unfit for any kind of service to him. Why not give them whereon to place their feet on an equal footing with the white children and made to work or starve; "to sink or swim; live or die; survive or perish?" What a noble motto that would be for them to adopt!

We then turn for our homeward trip, a distance of fifteen miles, but no one stops to count miles here, where roads could not be better.

When within six miles of Mr. Kuhn's, we stopped by invitation given in the morning, and took tea with Mrs. W., who received us with: "You don't know how much good it does me to have you ladies come!" Then led the way into her sod house, saying, "I wish we had our new house built, so we could entertain you better." But her house was more interesting to us with its floorless kitchen, and room covered with a neat rag carpet underlaid with straw. The room was separated from the kitchen by being a step higher, and two posts where the door would have been had the partition been finished.

The beds and chairs were of home manufacture, but the chairs were cushioned, and the beds neatly arranged with embroidered shams, and looked so comfortable that while the rest of the party prospected without, I asked to lie down and rest, and was soon growing drowsy with my comfortable position when Mrs. W. roused me with: "I cannot spare your company long enough for you to go to sleep. No one knows how I long for company; indeed, my very soul grows hungry at times for society."

Poor woman! she looked every word she spoke, and my heart went right out to her in pity, and I asked her to tell us her experience.

I will quote her words and tell her story, as it is the language and experience of many who come out from homes of comfort, surrounded by friends, to build up and regain their lost fortunes in the West. Mrs. W's. appearance was that of a lady of refinement, and had once known the comforts and luxuries of a good home in the East. But misfortunes overtook them, and they came to the West to regain what they had lost. Had settled there about three years before and engaged in stock raising. The first year the winter was long and severe, and many of their cattle died; but were more successful the succeeding years, and during the coming summer were ready to build a new house, not of sod, but of lumber.

"We had been thinking of leaving this country, but this colony settling here will help it so much, and now we will stay."

Her books of poems were piled up against the plastered wall, showing she had a taste for the beautiful.

After a very pleasant couple of hours we bade her good-bye, and made our last start for home. The only flowers found on the way were the buffalo beans and a couple of clusters of white flowers that looked like daisies, but are almost stemless. On our way we drove over a prairie dog town, frightening the little barkers into their underground homes.

Here and there a doggie sentinel kept his position on the roof of his house which is only a little mound, barking with a fine squeaky bark to frighten us away and warn others to keep inside; but did we but turn toward him and wink, he wasn't there any more.

Stopped for a few moments at the colony tent and found only about six of the family at home, including a gentleman from New Jersey who had joined them.

The day had been almost cloudless and pleasantly warm, and as we finished our journey it was made thrice beautiful by the setting sun, suggesting the crowning thought: will I have another May-day, and where?

Wednesday was pleasant, and I spent it writing letters and sending to many friends pressed leaves and flowers and my maying in Nebraska.

The remainder of the week was bright; but showery. "Wiggins" was kept hanging on a tree in the door yard, to be consulted with about storms, and he generally predicted one, and a shower would come. We did so want the rain to cease long enough for the river to fall that we might cross over on horseback to the other side and take a ramble over the bluffs of Dakota, and perhaps get a sight of a Sioux. As it kept so wet the colonists did not pitch their tents, and Mr. Kuhn's house was well filled with weather stayed emigrants.

Mr. and Mrs. Morrison, Mrs. Taylor, and Will came Tuesday. They had not come to any stopping place when darkness settled upon them Saturday night and the ladies slept in the buggy, and men under the wagon. When daylight came they found they were not far from the first house along the way where they spent Sunday. Monday they went to the Niobrara river and stopped at the little house at the bridge; and Tuesday finished the journey. Their faces were burnt with the sun and wind; but the ladies dosed them with sweet cream, which acted admirably. Mr. Taylor returned his horses to their former owner, bought a team of oxen, and left Stuart on Monday, but over-fed them, and was all the week coming with sick oxen. Mr. Barnwell's oxen stampeded one night and were not found for over a week. Such were the trials of a few of the N. M. A. C.

Perhaps you can learn from their experiences. I have already learned that, if possible, it is best to have your home selected, and a shelter prepared, and then bring your family and household goods. Bring what you really need, rather than dispose of it at a sacrifice. Do not expect to, anywhere, find a land of perpetual sunshine or a country just the same as the one you left. Do not leave Pa. expecting to find the same old "Keystone" in Nebraska; were it just the same you would not come. Expect disappointments and trials, and do not be discouraged when they come, and wish yourself "back to the good old home." Adopt for your motto, "What *others* have done *I* can do." Allow me to give you Mr. and Mrs. K.'s story; it will tell you more than any of the colonists can ever tell, as they have lived through the disadvantages of the first opening of this country. Mr. K. says: "April of '79 I came to this country to look up a home where I could have good cattle range. When we came to this spot we liked it and laid some logs crosswise to look like a foundation and mark the spot. Went further west, but returned and pitched our tent; and in a week, with the help of a young man who accompanied us, the kitchen part of our house was under roof. While we worked at the house Mrs. K. and our two girls made garden. We then returned thirty-five miles for our goods and stock, and came back in

May to find the garden growing nicely. Brought a two months' supply of groceries with us, as there was no town nearer than Keya Paha, thirty miles east at the mouth of the river; there in fact, was about the nearest house.

"Ours was the first house on the south side of the river, and I soon had word sent me by Spotted Tail, Chief of the Sioux, to get off his reservation. I told the bearer of his message to tell Mr. Spotted Tail, that I was not on his land but in Nebraska, and on surveyed land; so to come ahead. But was never disturbed in any way by the Indians, whose reservation lay just across the river. They often come, a number together, and want to trade clothing and blankets furnished them by the government, giving a blanket for a mere trinket or few pounds of meat, and would exchange a pony for a couple quarts of whisky. But it is worth more than a pony to put whisky into their hands, as it is strictly prohibited, and severely punished by law, as it puts them right on the war-path.

"The next winter a mail route was established, and our house was made Burton post-office, afterwards changed to Brewer. It was carried from Keya Paha here and on to the Rose Bud agency twice a week. After a time it was dropped, but resumed again, and now goes west to Valentine, a distance of about sixty miles.

"The nearest church and school was at Keya Paha.

Now we have a school house three miles away, where they also have preaching, the minister (M. E.) coming from Keya Paha."

Mrs. K. who is brave as woman can be, and knows well the use of firearms, says: "I have stayed for a week at a time with only Mr. K.'s father, who is blind and quite feeble, for company. Had only the lower part of our windows in then, and never lock our doors. Have given many a meal to the Indians, who go off with a "thank you," or a grunt of satisfaction. They do not always ask for a meal, but I generally give them something to eat as our cattle swim the river and graze on reservation lands. Anyway, kindness is never lost. My two daughters have gone alone to Keya Paha often. I have made the trip without meeting a soul on the way.

"The latch string of our door has always hung out to every one. The Indians would be more apt to disturb us if they thought we were afraid of them."

It was a real novelty and carried me back to my grandmother's days, to "pull the string and hear the latch fly up" on their kitchen door.

Their house, a double log, is built at the foot of the bluff and about seventy rods from the river, and is surrounded by quite a grove of burr oak and other trees. They came with twelve head of cattle and now have over eighty, which could command a good price did they wish to sell.

Thus, with sunshine and showers the week passes

quickly enough, and brought again the Sabbath bright and clear, but windy. A number of us took a walk one and one-half miles up the valley to the colony tent; went by way of a large oak tree, in the branches of which the body of an Indian chief had been laid to rest more than four years ago. From the bleached bones and pieces of clothing and blanket that were yet strewn about beneath the tree, it was evident he had been of powerful frame, and had been dressed in a coat much the same as a soldier's dress coat, with the usual decoration of brass buttons. Wrapped in his blanket and buffalo robe, he had been tied with thongs to the lower limbs, which were so low that the wolves had torn the body down.

When we reached the tent under which they had expected to hold their meetings and Sabbath-school, we found it, like many of their well-meant plans, now flat on the ground. It had come down amid the rain and wind of last night on the sleepers, and we found the tenters busy with needles trying to get it in order for pitching. None busier prodding their finger ends than was Mr. Clark.

"What have you been doing all this time, Mr. C.?" I asked.

"What have I been doing? Why it has just kept me busy to keep from drowning, blowing away, freezing, and starving to death. It is about all a man can attend to at one time. Haven't been idling any time away, I can tell you."

We felt sorry for the troubles of the poor men, but learned this lesson from their experience—never buy a tent so old and rotten that it won't hold to the fastenings, to go out on the prairies of Nebraska with; it takes good strong material to stand the wind.

In the afternoon we all went up on to the table-land to see the prairies burn. A great sheet of flame sweeping over the prairie is indeed a grand sight, but rather sad to see what was the tall waving grass of last year go up in a blaze and cloud of smoke only to leave great patches of blackened earth. Yet it is soon brightened by the new growth of grass which could not show itself for so long if the old was not burnt.

Some say it is necessary to burn the old grass off, and at the same time destroy myriads of grasshoppers and insects of a destructive nature, and also give the rattlesnake a scorching. While others say, burning year after year is hurtful to the soil, and burns out the grass roots; also that decayed vegetation is better than ashes for a sandy soil.

These fires have been a great hindrance to the growth of forest trees. Fire-brakes are made by plowing a number of furrows, which is often planted in corn or potatoes. I fancy I would have a good wide potato patch all round my farm if I had one, and never allow fire on it. To prevent being caught in a prairie fire, one should always carry a supply of matches. If a fire is seen coming, start a fire which of course will burn from you, and in a few minutes after the fire has passed over the ground, it can be walked over, and you soon have a cleared spot, where the fire cannot reach you.

Monday, 21st. Bright and pleasant, and Mr. K. finishes his corn planting.

A DESCRIPTION OF THE COUNTRY IN WHICH THE COLONY LOCATED.

As this is to be my last day here, I must tell you all there is yet to be told of this country. There are so many left behind that will be interested in knowing all about the country their friends have gone to, so I will try to be very explicit, and state clearly all I have learned and seen of it. Allow me to begin with the great range of bluffs that closely follow the north side of the river. We can only see their broken, irregular, steep, and sloping sides, now green with grass, on which cattle are grazing—that swim the river to pasture off the "Soo" (as Sioux is pronounced) lands. The reservation is very large, and as the agency is far west of this, they do not occupy this part much, only to now and then take a stroll over it.

The difference between a hill and a bluff is, that a bluff is only half a hill, or hill only on one side. The ground rises to a height, and then maintains that height for miles and miles, which is called table-land. Then comes the Keya Paha river, which here is the dividing line between Dakota and Nebraska.

It is 125 miles long. At its mouth, where it empties into the Niobrara, it is 165 feet wide. Here, thirty-five miles north-west, it is about 75 feet wide, and 6 feet deep. The water flows swiftly over its sandy bed, but Mr. K. says "there is rock bottom here." The sand is very white and clean, and the water is clear and pleasant to the taste.

The banks are fringed with bushes, principally willow. The valley on the south side is from one-fourth to one and one half-miles wide, and from the growth of grass and bushes would think the soil is quite rich. The timber is pine, burr oak, and cottonwood principally, while there are a few cedar, elm, ash, boxelder and basswood to be found. The oak, elm, and boxelder are about all I have seen, as the timber is hid in the canyons. Scarcely a tree to be seen on the table-lands. Wild plums, choke cherries, and grapes are the only fruits of the country. No one has yet attempted fruit culture. The plums are much the same in size and quality as our cultivated plums. They grow on tall bushes, instead of trees, and are so interwoven with the cherry bushes, and in blossom so much alike, I cannot tell plum from cherry bush. They both grow in great patches along the valley, and form a support for the grape vines that grow abundantly, which are much the same as the "chicken grapes" of Pennsylvania. I must not overlook the dwarf or sand-hill cherry, which, however, would not be a hard matter, were it not for the little white blossoms that cover the crooked little sticks, generally about a foot in height, that come up and spread in every direction. It is not choice of its bed, but seems to prefer sandy soil. Have been told they are pleasant to the taste and refreshing.

Then comes the wild gooseberry, which is used, but the wild black currants are not gathered. Both grow abundantly as does also the snowberry, the same we cultivate for garden shrubbery. Wild hops are starting up every where, among the bushes and ready to climb; are said to be equally as good as the poled hops of home.

"Beautiful wild flowers will be plenty here in a couple of weeks," Mrs. K. says, but I cannot wait to see them. The most abundant, now, is the buffalo bean, of which I have before spoken, also called ground plum, and prairie clover: plum from the shape of the pod it bears in clusters, often beautifully shaded with red, and prairie clover from the flower, that resembles a large clover head in shape, and often in color, shading from a dark violet to a pale pink, growing in clusters, and blooming so freely, it makes a very pretty prairie flower. It belongs to the pulse order, and the beans it bears can be cooked as ordinary beans and eaten—if at starvation point. Of the other flowers gathered mention was made on my May-day.

Mr. K. has a number of good springs of water on his farm, and it is easily obtained on the table-land. It cannot be termed soft water, yet not very hard.

About one-half of the land I am told is good tillable land, the other half too sandy for anything but pasture lands. Soil is from eighteen inches to two feet deep.

I will here quote some of the objections to the country offered by those who were not pleased. Time only can tell how correct they are. "It is too far north. Will never be a general farming or fruit growing country. Summer season will be too short for corn to ripen. Too spotted with sand hills to ever be thickly settled. Afraid of drouth. Too far from railroad and market, and don't think it will have a railroad nearer soon. Those Sioux are not pleasant neighbors. Winters will be long and cold." But all agree that it is a healthy country, and free from malaria. Others say, "Beautiful country. Not as cold as in Pennsylvania. Of course we can raise fruit; where wild fruit will grow tame fruit can be cultivated. Those sand hills are just what we want; no one will take them, and while our cattle are grazing on them, we will cultivate our farms." We feel like quoting a copy often set for us to scribble over when a little girl at school, with only a little alteration. "Many men of many minds, many lands of many kinds"—to scatter over—and away some have gone, seeking homes elsewhere.

Those who have remained are getting breaking done, and making garden and planting sod corn and potatoes, which with broom corn is about all they can raise on new ground the first summer. Next will come the building of their log and sod shanties, and setting out of their timber culture, which is done by plowing ten acres of ground and sticking in cuttings from the cottonwood, which grows readily and rapidly.

There are a few people scattered over the country who have engaged in stock raising, but have done little farming and improving. So you see it is almost untouched, and not yet tested as to what it will be as a general farming country. Years of labor and trials of these new-comers will tell the story of its worth.

I sincerely hope it will prove to be all that is good for their sake! I hide myself away from the buzz and hum of voices below, in the quiet of an upper room that I may tell you these things which have been so interesting to me to learn, and hope they may be interesting to read.

But here comes Lizzie saying, "Why, Sims, you look like a witch hiding away up here; do come down." And I go and take a walk with Mrs. K. down to see their cattle corral. The name of corral was so foreign I was anxious to know all about it. It is a square enclosure built of heavy poles, with sheds on the north and west sides with straw or grass roof for shelter, and is all the protection from the cold the cattle have during the winter. Only the milk cows are corraled during the summer nights. A little log stable for the horses completes the corral, while of course hay and straw are stacked near. Then she took me to see a dugout in the side of a hill, in a sheltered ravine, or draw, and surrounded by trees. It is not a genuine dugout, but enough of the real to be highly interesting to me. It was occupied by a middle-aged man who is Mr. K.'s partner in the stock business, and a French boy, their herder. The man was intelligent, and looked altogether out of place as he sat there in the gloom of the one little room, lighted only by a half window and the open door, and, too, he was suffering from asthma. I asked: "Do you not find this a poor house for an asthmatic?"

"No, I do not find that it has that effect; I am as well here as I was before I came west."

The room was about 10x12, and 6 feet high. The front of the house and part of the roof was built of logs and poles, and the rest was made when God made the hill. They had only made the cavity in which they lived, floor enough for the pole bed to stand on.

To me it seemed too lonely for any enjoyment except solitude—so far removed from the busy throngs of the world. But the greater part of the stockman's time is spent in out-door life, and their homes are only retreats for the night.

We then climbed the hill that I might have a last view of sunset on the Keya Paha. I cannot tell you of its beauty, as I gaze in admiration and wonder, for sun, moon, and stars, have all left their natural course, or else I am turned all wrong.

Tuesday. Another pleasant day. Mrs. K., whom

I have learned to regard as a dear friend, and I, take our last walk and talk together, going first to the grave of a granddaughter on the hill, enclosed with a railing and protected from the prairie wolves by pieces of iron. Oh! I thought, as I watched the tears course down Mrs. K's. cheek as she talked of her "darling," there is many a sacred spot unmarked by marble monument on these great broad plains of Nebraska. "You see there is no doctor nearer than Keya Paha, and by the time we got him here he could do her no good." Another disadvantage early settlers labor under.

Then to the river that I might see it flow for the last time, and gather sand and pebbles of almost every color that mingle with it. I felt it was my last goodbye to this country and I wished to carry as much of it away in my satchel and in memory as possible.

We then returned to the house, and soon Mr. Newell who was going to Stuart, came, and with whom I had made sure of a passage back. Mrs. K. and all insisted my stay was not near long enough, but letters had been forwarded to me from Stuart from brother C. asking me to join him. And Miss Cody, with whom I had been corresponding for some time, insisted on my being with her soon; so I was anxious to be on my way, and improved the first opportunity to be off. So, chasing Lizzie for a kiss, who declared, "I cannot say good-bye to Sims," and bidding them all a last farewell, with much surface merriment to hide sadness, and soon the little group of friends were left behind.

I wonder did they see through my assuming and know how sorry I was to part from them?—Mrs. K., who had been so kind, and the colony people all? I felt I had an interest in the battle that had already begun with them. Had I not anticipated a share of the battle and also of the spoils when I thought of being one with them. I did feel so sorry that the location was such that the majority had not been pleased, and our good plans could not be carried out.

It was not supposed as night after night the hall was crowded with eager anxious ones, that all would reach the land of promise. But even had those who come been settled together there would have been quite a nice settlement of people.

The territory being so spotted with sand hills was the great hindrance to a body of people settling down as the colony had expected to, all together as one settlement. One cannot tell, to look over it, just where the sandy spots are, as it is all covered with grass. They are only a slight raise in the ground and are all sizes, from one to many acres.

One-half section would be good claimable land, and other half no good. In some places I can see the sand in the road that drifts off the unbroken ground. We stopped for dinner at Mr. Newell's brother's, whose wife is a daughter of Mr. Kuhn's, and then the final start is made for the Niobrara. The country looks so different to me now as I return over the same road behind horses, and the sun is bright and warm. The tenters have gone to building log houses, and there are now four houses to be seen along the way. Am told most of the land is taken.

We pass close to one of the houses, where the husband is plowing and the wife dropping seed corn; and we stop for a few minutes, that I may learn one way of planting sod corn. The dropper walks after the plow and drops the corn close to the edge of the furrow, and it comes up between the edges of the sod. Another way is to cut a hole in the sod with an ax, and drop the corn in the hole, and step on it while you plant the next hill—I mean hole—of corn.

One little, lone, oak tree was all the tree seen along the road, and not a stone. I really miss the jolting of the stones of Pennsylvania roads. But strewed all along are pebbles, and in places perfect beds of them. I cannot keep my eyes off the ground for looking at them, and, at last, to satisfy my wishing for "a lot of those pretty pebbles to carry home," Mr. N. stops, and we both alight and try who can find the prettiest. As I gather, I cannot but wonder how God put these pebbles away up here!

Reader, if all this prairie land was waters, it would make a good sized sea, not a storm tossed sea but water in rolling waves. It looks as though it had been the bed of a body of water, and the water leaked out or ran down the Niobrara river, cutting out the canyons as it went, and now the sea has all gone to grass.

Mr. N. drives close to the edge of an irregular series of canyons that I may have a better view.

"I do wish you would tell me, Mr. N., how these canyons have been made?"

"Why, by the action of the wind and water."

"Yes, I suppose; but looks more like the work of an immense scoop-shovel, and all done in the dark; they are so irregular in shape, size, and depth."

Most that I see on this side of the river are dry, grassy, and barren of tree or bush, while off on the other side, can be seen many well filled with burr oak, pine, and cedar.

Views such as I have had from the Stone Butte, along the Keya Paha, on the broad plains, and now of the valley of the Niobrara well repays me for all my long rides, and sets my mind in a perfect query of how and when was all this wonderful work done? I hope I shall be permitted to some day come again, and if I cannot get over the ground any other way, I will take another ride behind oxen.

Several years ago these canyons afforded good hiding places for stray (?) ponies and horses that strayed from their owners by the maneuvering of "Doc." Middleton, and his gang of "pony boys," as those who steal or run off horses from the Indians are called. But they did not confine themselves to Indian ponies alone, and horses and cattle were stolen without personal regard for the owner.

But their leader has been safe in the penitentiary at Lincoln for some time, and the gang in part disbanded; yet depredations are still committed by them, which has its effect upon some of the colonists, who feel that they do not care to settle where they would be apt to lose their horses so unceremoniously. A one-armed traveler, who took shelter from the storm with a sick wife on the island, had one of his horses stolen last week, which is causing a good deal of indignation. Their favorite rendezvous before the band was broken was at "Morrison's bridge," where we spent the rainy Sabbath. Oh, dear! would I have laid me down so peacefully to sleep on the table that night had I known more of the history of the little house and the dark canyons about?

But the house has another keeper, and nothing remains but the story of other days to intimidate us now, and we found it neat and clean, and quite inviting after our long ride.

After supper I went out to take a good look at the Niobrara river, or *Running Water*. Boiling and surging, its muddy waves hurried by, as though it was over anxious to reach the Missouri, into which it empties. It has its source in Wyoming, and is 460 miles long. Where it enters the state, it is a clear, sparkling stream, only 10 feet wide; but by the time it gathers and rushes over so much sand, which it

6

keeps in a constant stir, changing its sand bars every few hours, it loses its clearness, and at this point is about 165 feet wide. Like the Missouri river, its banks are almost entirely of a dark sand, without a pebble. So I gathered sand again, and after quite a search, found a couple of little stones, same color of the sand, and these I put in my satchel to be carried to Pennsylvania, to help recall this sunset picture on the "Running Water," and, for a more substantial lean for memory I go with Mr. N. on to the island to look for a diamond willow stick to carry home to father for a cane. The island is almost covered with these tall willow bushes. The bridge was built about four years ago. The piers are heavy logs pounded deep into the sand of the river bed, and it is planked with logs, and bushes and sod. It has passed heavy freight trains bound for the Indian Agency and the Black Hills, and what a mingling of emigrants from every direction have paid their toll and crossed over to find new homes beyond! Three wagons pass by this evening, and one of the men stopped to buy milk from Mrs Slack "to make turnover cake;" and made enquiry, saying:

"Where is that colony from Pennsylvania located? We would like to get near it."

It is quite a compliment to the colony that so many come so far to settle near them; but has been quite a hindrance. Long before the colony arrived, people were gathering in and occupying the best of the land, and thus scattering the little band of colonists. Indeed the fame of the colony will people this country by many times the number of actual settlers it itself will bring.

Mrs. S. insists that I "give her some music on the organ," and I attempt "Home sweet, home," but my voice fails me, and I sing "Sweet hour of prayer," as more befitting. Home for me is not on the Niobrara, and in early morn we leave it to flow on just as before, and we go on toward Stuart, casting back good-bye glances at its strangely beautiful valley. The bluffs hug the river so close that the valley is not wide, but the canyons that cut into the bluffs help to make it quite an interesting picture.

There is not much more to be told about the country on the south side of the river. It is not sought after by the claim-hunters as the land on the north is. A few new houses can be seen, showing that a few are persuaded to test it.

The grass is showing green, and where it was burnt off on the north side of the valley, and was only black, barren patches a little more than a week ago, now are bright and green. A few new flowers have sprung up by the way-side. The sweetest in fragrance is what they call the wild onion. The root is the shape and taste of an onion, and also the stem when bruised has quite an onion smell; but the tiny, pale pink flower reminds me of the old May pinks for fragrance. Another tiny flower is very much like mother's treasured pink oxalis; but is only the bloom of wood sorrel. It opens in morning and closes at evening, and acts so much like the oxalis, I could scarcely be persuaded it was not; but the leaves convinced me.

I think the setting sun of Nebraska must impart some of its rays to the flowers, that give them a different tinge; and, too, the flowers seem to come with the leaves, and bloom so soon after peeping through the sod. The pretty blue and white starlike iris was the only flower to be found about Stuart when I left.

We have passed a number of emigrant wagons, and—"Oh, horror! Mr. Newell, look out for the red-skins!"

"Where, Miss Fulton, where?"

"Why there, on the wagon and about it, and see, they are setting fire to the prairie; and oh dear! one of them is coming toward us with some sort of a weapon in his hand. Guess I'll wrap this bright red Indian blanket around me and perhaps they will take me for a 'Soo' and spare me scalp."

Reader I have a mind to say "continued in the next" or "subscribe for the Ledger and read the rest," but that would be unkind to leave you in suspense, though I fear you are growing sleepy over this the first chapter even, and I would like to have some thrilling adventure to wake you up.

But the "Look out for the red skins," was in great

red letters on a prairie schooner, and there they were, men with coats and hats painted a bright red, taking their dinner about a fire which the wind is trying to carry farther, and one is vigorously stamping it out. Another, a mere boy with a stick in his hand, comes to inquire the road to the bridge "where you don't have to pay toll?" Poor men, they look as though they had'nt ten cents to spare. So ends my adventure with the "red skins." But here comes another train of emigrants; ladies traveling in a covered carriage, while the horses, cattle, people, and all show they come from a land of plenty, and bring a goodly share of worldly goods along.

They tell Mr. N. they came from Hall county, Nebraska, where vegetation is at least two weeks ahead of this country, but came to take up government land. So it is, some go with nothing, while others sell good homes and go with a plenty to build up another where they can have the land for the claiming of it.

The sun has not been so bright, and the wind is cool and strong, but I have been well protected by this thick warm Indian blanket, yet I am not sorry when I alight at Mr. Skirvings door and receive a hearty welcome, and "just in time for a good dinner."

THE COLONISTS FIRST SUMMER'S WORK AND HARVEST.

It would not do to take the colonists to their homes on the frontier, and not tell more of them.

I shall copy from letters received. From a letter

received from one whom I know had nothing left after reaching there but his pluck and energy, I quote:

"BREWER, P. O. BROWN CO., NEB.,
"December 23, '83.

"Our harvest has been good. Every man of the colony is better satisfied than they were last spring, as their crops have done better than they expected. My sod corn yielded 20 bushels (shelled) per acre. Potatoes 120 bushels. Beans 5, and I never raised larger vegetables than we did this summer on sod. On old ground corn 40, wheat 20 to 35, and oats 40 to 60 bushels per acre. After the first year we can raise all kinds of grain. For building a sod house, it costs nothing besides the labor, but for the floor, doors and windows. I built one to do me for the summer, and was surprised at the comfort we took in it; and now have a log house ready for use, a sod barn of two rooms, one for my cow, and the other for the chickens and ducks, a good cave, and a well of good water at eight feet.

"There are men in the canyons that take out building logs. They charge from twenty-five to thirty-five dollars per forty logs, sixteen and twenty feet long. To have these logs hauled costs two and two and one-half dollars per day, and it takes two days to make the trip. But those who have the time and teams can do their own hauling and get their own logs, as the trees belong to "Uncle Sam."

"The neighbors all turn out and help at the raising

The timber in the canyons are mostly pine. Our first frost was 24th September, and our first cold weather began last week. A number of the colonists built good frame houses. I have been offered $600.00 for my claims, but I come to stay, and stay I will."

From another:

"We are all in good health and like our western homes. Yet we have some drawbacks; the worst is the want of society, and fruit, Are going to have a reunion 16 February."

"Brewer, Jan., 8.

"You wished to know what we can do in the winter. I have been getting wood, and sitting by the fire. Weather beautiful until 15th December, but the thermometer has said "below zero," ever since Christmas. The lowest was twenty degrees. The land is all taken around here (near the Stone Butte) and we expect in a couple of years to have schools and plenty of neighbors."

Those who located near Stuart and Long Pine, are all doing well, and no sickness reported from climating.

I have not heard of one being out of employment. One remarked: "This is a good country for the few of us that came."

I believe that the majority of the first party took claims; but the little handful of colonists are nothing in number to the settlers that have gathered in from everywhere, and occupy the land with them. Of the horse thieves before spoken of I would add, that the "vigilantes" have been at work among them, hanging a number to the nearest tree, and lodging a greater number in jail.

It is to be hoped that these severe measures will be all sufficient to rid the country of these outlaws. May the "colonists" dwell in peace and prosperity, and may the harvest of the future prove rich in all things good!

CHAPTER II.

Over the Sioux City & Pacific R. R. from Valentine to the Missouri Valley. A visit to Ft. Niobrara.

I was advised to go to Valentine, the present terminus of the S. C. & P. R. R., and also to visit Fort Niobrara only a few miles from Valentine, as I would find much that was interesting to write about. Long Pine was also spoken of as a point of interest, and as Mr. Buchanan, Gen. Pass. Agt. of the road, had so kindly prepared my way by sending letters of introduction to Lieut. Davis, quartermaster at the Fort, and also to the station agent at Valentine, I felt I would not give it up as others advised me to, as Valentine is considered one of the wicked places of Nebraska, on account of the cow boys of that neighborhood making it their head-quarters.

I had been so often assured of the respect the cow boys entertain for ladies, that I put aside all fears, and left on a freight train, Friday evening, May 25th, taking Mrs. Peck, a quiet middle-aged lady with me for company. Passenger trains go through Stuart at night, and we availed ourselves of the freight caboose in order to see the country by daylight. A quiet looking commercial agent, and a "half-breed" who busies himself with a book, are the only passengers besides Mrs. Peck and I. There is not much to tell of this country. It is one vast plain with here a house, and there a house, and here and there a house, and that's about all; very little farming done, no trees, no bushes, no nothing but prairie.

There, the cars jerk, jerk, jerk, and shake, shake, shake! Must be going up grade! Mrs. P. is fat, the agent lean and I am neither; but we all jerk, shake and nod. Mrs. P. holds herself to the chair, the agent braces himself against the stove, and I—well I just shake and laugh. It isn't good manners, I know, but Mrs. P. looks so frightened, and the agent so queer, that my facial muscles will twitch; so I hide my face and enjoy the fun. There, we are running smooth now. Agent remarks that his wife has written him of a terrible cyclone in Kansas City last Sunday. Cyclone last Sunday! What if it had passed along the Niobrara and upset the little house with all aboard into the river. One don't know when to be thankful, do they?

Newport and Bassett are passed, but they are only mere stations, and not worthy the name of town. The Indian has left our company for that of the train-men, and as Mrs. P.'s husband is a merchant, and she is prospecting for a location for a store, she and the agent, who seems quite pleasant, find plenty to talk about. There, puffing up grade again! and the jerking, nodding and shaking begins. Mrs. P. holds her head, the agent tries to look unconcerned, and as though he didn't shake one bit, and I just put my head out of the window, and watch the country.

Saw three antelope running at a distance; are smaller than deer.

The land is quite level, but we are seldom out of sight of sand-hills or bluffs. Country looks better and more settled as we near Long Pine, where several of the colonists have located, and I have notified them of our coming, and there! I see a couple of them coming to the depot to meet us. As the sun has not yet hid behind the "Rockies," we proposed a walk to Long Pine creek, not a mile away. The tops of the tallest trees that grow along it, tower just enough above the table-land to be seen from the cars; and as we did not expect to stop on our return, we made haste to see all we could. But by the time we got down to the valley it was so dark we could only see enough to make us very much wish to see more. So we returned disappointed to the hotel, to wait for the regular passenger train, which was not due until about midnight. The evening was being pleasantly passed with music and song, when my eyes rested upon a couple of pictures that hung on the wall, and despite the company about me, I was carried over a bridge of sad thoughts to a home where pictures of the same had hung about a little bed, and in fancy I am tucking little niece "Myrtle" away for the night, after she has repeated her evening prayer to me, and I hear her say:

"Oh! auntie! I forgot to say, "God bless everybody."

The prayer is repeated, good-night kisses given, and "Mollie doll" folded close in her arms to go to sleep, too. But the sweet voice is silent now, " Mollie" laid away with the sacred playthings, the playful hands closer folded, and the pictures look down on me, far, so far from home; and I leave the singers to their songs while I think.

To add to my loneliness, Mrs. P. says she is afraid to venture to Valentine, and I do not like to insist, lest something might occur, and the rest try to persuade me not to go. I had advised Lieut. Davis of my coming, and he had written me to telephone him on my arrival at the depot, and he would have me conveyed to the Fort immediately.

But better than all, came the thought, "the Lord, in whose care and protection I left home, has carried me safe and well this far; cannot I trust Him all the way?" My faith is renewed, and I said:

"You do not need to go with me, Mrs. P., I can go alone. The Lord has always provided friends for me when I was in need of them, and I know He will not forsake me now."

Mrs. P. hesitated, but at last, gathering strength from my confidence, says:

"Well, I believe I will go, after all."

"Almost train time," the landlady informs us, and we all go down to the depot to meet it. The night is clear and frosty, and the moon just rising.

The train stopped for some time, and we talked of colony matters until our friends left us, insisting that we should stop on our return, and spend Sunday at Long Pine.

I turn my seat, and read the few passengers. Just at my back a fat, fatherly looking old gentleman bows his head in sleep. That gentleman back of Mrs. P. looks so thoughtful. How attentive that gentleman across the aisle is to that aged lady! Suppose she is his dear old mother!

"Why there is 'Mr. Agent!' and there—well, I scarcely know what that is in the back seat." A bushy head rests against the window, and a pair of red shoes swings in the aisle from over the arm of the seat. But while I look at the queer picture, and wonder what it is, it spits a great splash of tobacco juice into the aisle, and the query is solved, it's only a man. Always safe in saying there is a man about when you see tobacco juice flying like that. Overalls of reddish brown, coat of gray, face to match the overalls in color, and hair to match the coat in gray, while a shabby cap crowns the picture that forms our background.

Mr. Agent tells the thoughtful man a funny story. The old lady wakes up, and the fatherly old gent rouses.

"You ladies belong to the colony from Pennsylvania, do you not?" he asked.

"I am a member of the colony," I replied.

"I am glad to have an opportunity to enquire about them; how are they getting along?"

I gave him all the information I could, and soon all were conversing as lonely travelers will, without waiting for any ceremonial introductions. But soon "Ainsworth" is called out, and the agent leaves us with a pleasant "good evening" to all. The elderly man proves to be J. Wesley Tucker, Receiver at the United States Land office, at Valentine, but says it is too rough and bad to take his family there, and tells stories of the wild shooting, and of the cow-boy. The thoughtful man is Rev. Joseph Herbert, of Union Park Seminary, Chicago, who will spend his vacation in preaching at Ainsworth and Valentine, and this is his first visit to Valentine, and is the first minister that has been bold enough to attempt to hold services there. He asks; "Is the colony supplied with a minister? The superintendent of our mission talks of sending one to them if they would wish it."

"They have no minister, and are feeling quite lost without preaching, as nearly all are members of some church, and almost every denomination is represented; but I scarcely know where services could be held; no church and no school house nearer than three miles."

"Oh! we hold services in log or sod houses, anywhere we can get the people together."

I then spoke of my mission of writing up the history of the colony, and their settling, and the country they located in, and why I went to Valentine, and remarked:

"I gathered some very interesting history from—"

"Well if you believe all old——tells you, you may just believe everything," came from the man in the back-ground, who had not ventured a word before, and with this he took a seat nearer the rest of us, and listened to Mr. T. telling of the country, and of the utter recklessness and desperation of the cow-boys; how they shot at random, not caring where their bullets flew, and taking especial delight in testing the courage of strangers by the "whiz of the bullets about their ears."

"Is there any place where I can stop and go back, and not go on to Valentine," I asked.

"No, Miss, you are bound for Valentine now;" and added for comfort sake, "no danger of you getting shot, *unless* by *mere accident*. They are very respectful to ladies, in fact, are never known to insult a lady. Pretty good hearted boys when sober, but when they are on a spree, they are as *wild* as *wild* can be;" with an ominous shake of his head.

"Do you think they will be on a spree when I get there?"

"Can't say, indeed; *hope not.*"

"A man came not long ago, and to test his courage or see how high he could jump, they shot about his feet and cut bullet holes through his hat, and the poor fellow left, not waiting to pick up his overcoat and baggage. A woman is carrying a bullet in her arm now where a stray one lodged that came through the house.

After this bit of information was delivered, he went into the other car to take a smoke. I readily understood it was more for his own amusement than ours that he related all this, and that he enjoyed emphasizing the most important words. The gentlemen across the aisle handed me his card with:

"I go on the same errand that you do, and visit the chaplain of the Fort, so do not be alarmed, that gentleman was only trying to test your courage."

I read the card: P. D. McAndrews, editor of Storm Lake *Tribune*, Storm Lake, Iowa. The minister looked interested, but only remarked:

"I fear no personal harm, the only fear I have is that I may not be able to do them as much good as others of more experience could."

I thought if any one needed to have fear, it was he, as his work would be among them. Mrs. P. whispered:

"Oh! is'nt it awful, are you alarmed?"

"Not as much as I appear to be, the gentleman evidently enjoyed teasing us, and I enjoyed seeing him so amused. We will reach there after sunrise and go as soon as we can to the Fort; we will not stop to learn much of Valentine, I know all I care to now."

The stranger, who by this time I had figured out as a pony boy—I could not think what else would give him such a countenance as he wore—changed the subject with:

"That man," referring to Judge T., "don't need to say there is no alkali along here, I freighted over this very country long before this railroad was built, and the alkali water has made the horses sick many a time. But I suppose it is wearing out, as the country has changed a good bit since then; there wasn't near as much grass growing over these sand hills then as there is now,"

Then by way of an apology for his appearnace, remarked:

"I tell you freighting is hard on a man, to drive day after day through all kinds of weather and sleep out at night soon makes a fellow look old. I look to be fifty, and I am only thirty-five years old. My folks all live in Ohio, and I am the only one from the old home."

Poor man! I thought, is that what gives you such a hardened expression; and I have been judging you so harshly.

"The only one from the old home," had a tone of sadness that set me to thinking, and I pressed my face close to the window pane, and had a good long think all to myself, while the rest dropped off to sleep. Is there not another aboard this train who is the only one away from the old home? And all alone, too. Yet I feel many dear ones are with me in heart, and to-night dear father's voice trembled as he breathed an evening benediction upon his children, and invokes the care and protection of Him who is

God over all upon a daughter, now so far beyond the shelter of the dear old home; while a loving mother whispers a fervent "amen." By brothers and sisters I am not forgotten while remembering their own at the altar, nor by their little ones; and in fancy I see them, white robed for bed, sweetly lisping, "God bless auntie Pet, and bring her safe home." And ever lifting my own heart in prayer for protection and resting entirely upon God's mercy and goodness, I go and feel I am not *alone.* | Had it not been for my faith in the power of prayer, I would not have undertaken this journey; but I thought as I looked up at the bright moon, could one of your stray beams creep in at mother's window, and tell her where you look down upon her daughter to-night, would it be a night of sleep and rest to her? I was glad they could rest in blissful ignorance, and I would write and tell them all about it when I was safe back. Of course I had written of my intended trip, but they did not know the character of Valentine, nor did I until I was about ready to start. But I knew Mr. Buchanan would not ask me to go where it was not proper I should go. So gathering all these comforting thoughts together, I rested, but did not care to sleep, for—

>Oh, moon! 'tis rest by far more sweet,
>To feast upon thy loveliness, than sleep.

Humming Ten thousand (or 1,500) miles away, Home, sweet home, and the Lord's Prayer to the same air, I keep myself company.

It was as bright and beautiful as night could be. The broad plains were so lit up I could see far away over a rolling prairie and sand-hills glistening in the frosty air; while many lakelets made a picture of silvery sheen I had never looked upon before. The moon peeped up at me from its reflection in their clear waters, and I watched it floating along, skipping from lakelet to lakelet, keeping pace alongside as though it, too, was going to preach in or write up Valentine, and was eager to be there with the rest of us. It was a night too lovely to waste in sleep, so I waked every moment of it until the sun came up and put the moon and stars out, and lit up the great sandy plains, with a greater light that changed the picture to one not so beautiful, but more interesting from its plainer view.

It is beyond the power of my pen to paint the picture of this country as I saw it in the early morning light, while standing at the rear door of the car. Through sand-cuts, over sand-banks, and now over level grassy plains. The little rose bushes leafing out, ready to bloom, and sticking out through the sandiest beds they could find. Where scarcely anything else would think of growing were tiny bushes of sand-cherries, white with blossoms. It seemed the picture was unrolled from beneath the wheels on a great canvas while we stood still; but the cars fairly bounded over the straight, level road until about six o'clock, when "Valentine," rings through the car, and Judge

Tucker cautioned me to "get ready to die," and we land at Valentine. He and Rev. Herbert went to breakfast at a restaurant (the only public eating house, meals 50 cents), and Mr. McAndrew, his mother, Mrs. P., and I went into the depot, and lost no time in telephoning to the Fort that there were four passengers awaiting the arrival of the ambulance, and then gathered about the stove to warm. Finding there was little warmth to be had from it, Mrs. P. and I thought we would take a walk about the depot in the bright sun. But I soon noticed a number of men gathered about a saloon door, and fearing they might take my poke hat for a target, I told Mrs. P. I thought it was pleasanter if not warmer inside. I seated myself close to that dear old Scotch lady, whom I felt was more of a protection to me than a company of soldiers would be. All was quiet at first, but as there is no hotel in Valentine, the depot is used as a resting place by the cow boys, and a number of them came in, but all quiet and orderly, and only gave us a glance of surprise and wonder. Not one bold, impudent stare did we receive from any one of them, and soon all fears were removed, and I quietly watched them. One whom I would take to be a ranch owner, had lodged in the depot, and came down stairs laughing and talking, with an occasional profane word, of the fun of the night before. He was a large, red-faced young looking man, with an air of ownership and authority; and the boys seemed to go to him for their orders, which were given in a brotherly sort of way, and some were right off to obey. All wore leather leggings, some trimmed with fur; heavy boots, and great spurs clanking; their leather belt of revolvers, and dirk, and the stockman's sombrero. Some were rather fine looking in features, but all wore an air of reckless daring rather than of hardened wickedness. One who threw himself down to sleep on an improvised bed on the seats in the waiting room, looked only a mere boy in years, rather delicate in features, and showed he had not been long at the life he was now leading; and it was evident he had once known a better life.

Another, equally as young in years, showed a much more hardened expression; yet he, too, looked like a run-away from a good home.

One poor weather-beaten boy came in and passed us without turning his head, and I thought him an old gray-headed man, but when I saw his face I knew he could not be more than twenty-five. He seemed to be a general favorite that was about to leave them, for, "I'm sorry you are going away, Jimmie," "You'll be sure to write to us, Jimmie, and let us know how you get along down there," and like expressions came from a number. I did not hear a profane word or rough expression from anyone, excepting the one before spoken of. I watched them closely, trying to read them, and thought: "Poor boys! where are your mothers, your sisters, your homes?" for theirs is a life that knows no home, and so often their life has a violent ending, going out in the darkness of a wild misspent life.

As the ambulance would not be there for some time, and I could not think of breakfasting at the restaurant, Mrs. P. and I went to a store and got some crackers and cheese, on which we breakfasted in the depot. Then, tired and worn out from my night of watching, and all fear banished, I fell asleep with my head resting on the window-sill; but was soon aroused by Rev. Herbert coming in to ask us if we wished to walk about and see the town.

The town site is on a level stretch of land, half surrounded by what looks to be a beautiful natural wall, broken and picturesque with gray rocks and pine trees.

It is a range of high bluffs that at a distance look to be almost perpendicular, that follow the north side of the Minnechaduza river, or Swift Running water, which flows south-east, and is tributary to the Niobrara. The river is so much below the level of the table-land that it can not be seen at a distance, so it was only a glimpse we obtained of this strange beauty. But for your benefit we give the description of it by another whose time was not so limited. "The view on the Minnechaduza is as romantic and picturesque as many of the more visited sights of our country. Approaching it from the south, when within about 100 yards of the stream the level plain on which Valentine is built is broken by numerous deep ravines with stately pines growing on their steep sides. Looking from the point of the bluffs, the stream flowing in a serpentine course, and often doubling upon itself, appears a small amber colored rivulet. Along the valley, which is about one-half mile wide, there are more or less of pine and oak. The stumps speak of a time when it was thickly wooded. The opposite banks or bluffs, which are more than 100 feet higher than those on the south, are an interesting picture. There are just enough trees on them to form a pretty landscape without hiding from view the rugged cliffs on which they grow. The ravines that cut the banks into sharp bluffs and crags are lost to view in their own wanderings."

Valentine, I am told, is the county seat of Cherry county, which was but lately organized. Last Christmas there was but one house on the town site, but about six weeks ago the railroad was completed from Thatcher to this point, and as Thatcher was built right amid the sand banks near the Niobrara river, the people living there left their sandy homes and came here; and now there is one hardware, one furniture, and two general stores; a large store-house for government goods for the Sioux Indians, a newspaper, restaurant, and five saloons, a hotel and number of houses in course of erection, also the United States land office of the Minnechaduza district, that includes the government land of Brown, Cherry, and Sioux counties. In all I counted about twenty-five houses, and three tents that served as houses. But this is not to be the terminus of the Sioux City and Pacific Railroad very long, as it, too, is "going west," just where is not known.

About eight o'clock a soldier boy in blue came with the ambulance, and returning to the depot for my satchel and ulster, which I had left there in the care of no one, but found all safe, our party of four bade Rev. Herbert good-bye and left him to his work with our most earnest wishes for his success. He had already secured the little restaurant, which was kept by respectable people, to hold services in.

From Valentine we could see Frederick's peak, and which looked to be but a short distance away. When we had gone about two miles in that direction the driver said if we were not in haste to reach the fort he would drive out of the way some distance that we might have a better view of it; and after going quite a ways, halted on an eminence, and then we were yet several miles from it. It is a lone mound or butte that rears a queerly capped point high above all other eminences around it. At that distance, it looked to be almost too steep to be climbed, and crowned with a large rounding rock. I was wishing I could stop over Sunday at the fort, as I found my time would be too limited, by even extending it to Monday, to get anything like a view, or gather any information of the country. But Mrs. P. insisted on returning that afternoon rather than to risk her life one night so near the Indians.

The ride was interesting, but very unpleasant from a strong wind that was cold and cutting despite the bright sun. I had fancied I would see a fort such as they had in "ye olden times"—a block house with loop-holes to shoot through at the Indians. But instead I found Fort Niobrara more like a pleasant little village of nicely built houses, most of them of a dobie brick, and arranged on three sides of a square. The officers' homes on the south side, all cottage houses, but large, handsomely built, and commodious. On the east are public buildings, chapel, library, lecture room, hall for balls and entertainments, etc. Along the north are the soldiers' buildings; eating, sleeping, and reading rooms; also separate drinking and billiard rooms for the officers and privates.

The drinking and playing of the privates, at least are under restrictions; nothing but beer is allowed them, and betting is punished. On this side is the armory, store-houses of government goods, a general store, tailor, harness, and various shops. At the rear of the buildings are the stables—one for the gray and another for the sorrel horses—about one hundred of each, and also about seventy-five mules.

The square is nicely trimmed and laid out in walks and planted in small trees, as it is but four years since the post, as it is more properly termed, was established. It all looked very pleasant, and I asked the driver if, as a rule, the soldiers enjoyed the life. He answered that it was a very monotonous life, as it is seldom they are called out to duty, and they are only wishing the Indians would give them a chance at a skirmish. The privates receive thirteen dollars per month, are boarded and kept in clothing. Extra work receives extra pay; for driving to the depot once every day, and many days oftener, he received fifteen cents per day. Those of the privates who marry and bring their wives there—and but few are allowed that privilege—do so with the understanding that their wives are expected to cook, wash, or sew for the soldiers in return for their own keeping.

After a drive around the square, Mr. McA. and mother alighted at the chaplain's, and Mrs. P. and I at Lieutenant G. B. Davis', and were kindly received by both Mr. and Mrs. Davis, but the Lieutenant was soon called away to engage in a cavalry drill, or sham battle; but Mrs. D. entertained us very pleasantly, which was no little task, as I never was so dull and stupid as I grew to be after sitting for a short time in their cosy parlor. How provoking to be so, when there was so much of interest about me, and my time so limited.

Mrs. D. insisted on my lying down and taking some rest, which I gladly consented to do, providing they would not allow me to sleep long. I quickly fell into a doze, and dreamt the Indians were coming over the bluffs to take the fort, and in getting away from them I got right out of bed, and was back in the parlor in less than ten minutes.

Mrs. D. then proposed a walk to some of the public buildings; but we were driven back by a gust of wind and rain, that swept over the bluffs that hem them in on the north-west, carrying with it a cloud of sand and dust. The clouds soon passed over, and we started over to see the cavalry drill, but again were driven back by the rain, and we watched the cavalrymen trooping in, after the battle had been fought, the greys in one company, and sorrels in another.

There were only about 200 soldiers at the post. The keeping up of a post is a great cost, yet it is a needed expense, as the knowledge of the soldiers being so near helps to keep the Indians quiet. Yet I could not see what would hinder them from overpowering that little handful of soldiers, despite their two gatling guns, that would shoot 1,000 Indians per minute, if every bullet would count, if they were so disposed. But they have learned that such an outbreak would be retaliated by other troops, and call down the indignation of their sole keeper and support—"Uncle Sam."

We were interested in hearing Lieut. Davis speak in words of highest praise of Lieut. Cherry, whose death in 1881 was so untimely and sad, as he was soon to bear a highly estimable young lady away from near my own home as a bride, whom he met at Washington, D. C., in '79, where he spent a portion of a leave of absence granted him in recognition of brave and conspicuous services at the battle of the Little Big Horn, known as Custer's massacre. He was a graduate of West Point, was a brave, intelligent, rising young officer. Not only was he a good soldier, but also a man of upright life, and his untimely and violent death brought grief to many hearts, and robbed the world of a good man and a patriot. As the story of his death, and what it led to is interesting, I will briefly repeat it:

Some time before this event happened, there were good grounds for believing that there was a band formed between some of the soldiers and rough characters about the fort to rob the paymaster, but it became known, and a company was sent to guard him from Long Pine. Not long after this a half-breed killed another in a saloon row, near the fort, and Lieut. Cherry was detailed to arrest the murderer. Lieut. C. took with him a small squad of soldiers, and two Indian scouts. When they had been out two days, the murderer was discovered in some rock fastnesses, and as the Lieutenant was about to secure him, he was shot by one of the soldiers of the squad by the name of Locke, in order to let the fugitive escape. The murderer of Lieut. C. escaped in the confusion that followed, but Spotted Tail, chief of the Sioux Indians, who held the lieutenant in great esteem, ordered out a company of spies under Crow Dog, one of his under chiefs, to hunt him down. They followed his trail until near Fort Pierre, where they found him under arrest. They wanted to bring him back to Fort Niobrara, but were not allowed to. He was tried and paid the penalty of life for life — a poor return for such a one as he had taken.

He was evidently one of the band before mentioned, but ignorant of this the lieutenant had chosen him to be a help, and instead was the taker of his life.

When Crow Dog returned without the murderer of Lieut. C., Spotted Tail was very angry, and put him under arrest. Soon after, when the Indians were about to start on their annual hunt, Spotted Tail would not let Crow Dog go, which made the feud still greater. In the fall, when Spotted Tail was about to start to Washington to consult about the agency lands, Crow Dog had his wife drive his wagon up to Spotted Tail's tepee, and call him out, when Crow Dog, who lay concealed in the wagon, rose up and shot him, and made his escape, but was so closely followed that after three days he came into Fort Niobrara, and gave himself up. He has been twice tried, and twice sentenced to death, but has again been granted a new trial, and is now a prisoner at Fort Pierre.

The new county is named Cherry in honor of the beloved lieutenant.

While taking tea, we informed Lieut. Davis that it was our intention to return on a combination train that would leave Valentine about 3 o'clock. Finding we would then have little time to reach the train, he immediately ordered the ambulance, and telephoned to hold the train a half hour our for arrival, as it was then time for it to leave. And bidding our kind entertainers a hasty good bye, we were soon on our way. Although I felt I could not do Fort Niobrara and the strange beauty of the surrounding country justice by cutting my visit so short, yet I was glad to be off on a day train, as the regular passenger train left after night, and my confidence in the cow boys and the rough looking characters seen on the street, was not sufficiently established by their quiet demeanor of the morning to fancy meeting a night train. The riddled sign-boards showed that there was a great amount of ammunition used there, and we did not care to have any of it used on us, or our good opinion of them spoiled by a longer stay, and, too, we wanted to have a daylight view of the country from there to Long Pine. So we did not feel sorry to see the driver lash the four mules into a gallop. At the bridge, spanning the Niobrara, we met Rev. Herbert and a couple of others on their way to the fort, who told us they thought the train had already started; but the driver only urged the mules to a greater speed, and as I clung to the side of the ambulance, I asked:

"Do mules ever run off?"

"Sometimes they do."

"Well, do you think that is what these mules are doing now?"

"No, I guess not."

And as if to make sure they would, he reached out and wielded the long lash whip, and we understood that he not only wished to make the train on time, but also show us how soldier boys can drive "government mules." The thought that they were mules of the "U. S." brand did not add to our ease of mind any, for we had always heard them quoted as the very worst of mules.

Mrs. P. shook her head, and said she did believe they were running off, and I got in a good position to make a hasty exit if necessary, and then watched them run. After all we enjoyed the ride of four and a half miles in less than 30 minutes, and thanked the driver for it as he helped us into the depot in plenty of time for the train.

Mr. Tucker brought us some beautiful specimens of petrified wood—chips from a petrified log, found along the Minnechaduza, as a reminder of our trip to Valentine. Several cow boys were in the depot, but as quiet as in the morning.

I employed the time in gathering information about the country from Mr. T. He informed me there was some good table-land beyond the bluffs, which would be claimed by settlers, and in a couple of years the large cattle ranches would have to go further west to find herding ground. They are driven westward just as the Indians and buffalo are, by the settling up of the country.

Valentine is near the north boundary of the state, is west of the 100th meridian, and 295 miles distant from the Missouri river.

When about ready to start, who should come to board the train but the man whom I thought must be a pony boy.

"Oh, Mrs. P.! that bad man is going too, and see! We will have to travel in only a baggage car!"

"Well, we cannot help ourselves now. The ambulance has started back, and we cannot stay here, so we are compelled to go."

Mr. T. remarked:

"He does look like a bad man; but don't you know you make your own company very often, and I am assured you will be well treated by the train-men, and even that bad-looking man; and to help you all I can, I will speak to the conductor in your behalf.

The two chairs of the coach were placed at our use, while the conductor and stranger occupied the tool-chest. One side-door was kept open that I might sit back and yet have a good view. Mrs. P., not in the least discomforted by our position, was soon nodding in her chair, and I felt very much alone.

"Where music is, his Satanic majesty cannot enter," I thought, and as I sat with book and pencil in hand, writing a few words now and then, I sang—just loud enough to be heard, many of the good old hymns and songs, and ended with, "Dreaming of home." I wanted to make that man think of "home and mother," if he ever had any. Stopping now and then to ask him some question about the country in the most respectful way, and as though he was the only one who knew anything about it, and was always answered in the most respectful manner.

I sat near the door, and was prepared to jump right out into a sand-bank if anything should happen; but nothing occurred to make any one jump, only Mrs. P., when I gave her a pinch to wake her up and whisper to her "to please keep awake for I feel dreadful lonely."

Well, all I got written was:

Left Valentine about 3:30 in a baggage and mail car, over the sandy roads, now crossing the Niobrara bridge 200 feet long, 108 feet high; river not wide; no timber to be seen; now over a sand fill and through a sand cut 101 feet deep, and 321 feet wide at top, and 20 at bottom. Men are kept constantly at work to remove the sand that drifts into the cuts.

THATCHER, seven miles from V., a few faces peer up at the train from their dug-out homes, station house, and one 8x10 deserted store-house almost entirely covered with the signs, "Butter, Vegetables, and Eggs," out of which, I am told, thousands of dollars' worth have been sold. Think it must have been canned goods, for old tin fruit cans are strewn all around.

To our right is a chain of sand hills, while to the left it is a level grassy plain. The most of these lakelets, spoken of before, I am told, are only here during rainy seasons. Raining most of the time now.

ARABIA, one house, and a tent that gives it an Arabic look.

WOOD LAKE, one house. Named from a lakelet and one tree. Some one has taken a claim here, and built a sod house. Beyond this there is scarcely a house to be seen.

JOHNSTOWN, two houses, a tent, and water tank. Country taking on a better appearance—farm houses dotting the country in every direction. Country still grows better as we near Ainsworth, a pretty little town, a little distance to the left. Will tell you of this place again.

Crossing the Long Pine Creek, one mile west of Long Pine town, we reach Long Pine about six o'clock.

Mrs. P. says she does not care to go the rest of the way alone, so I have concluded to stop there over Sabbath. I feel like heaping praises and thanks upon these men who have so kindly considered our presence. Not even in their conversation with each other have I noticed the use of one slang or profane word, and felt like begging pardon of the stranger for thinking so wrongly of him.

Allow me to go back and tell you of Ainsworth:

Ainsworth is located near Bone creek, on the homestead of Mrs. N. J. Osborne, and Mr. Hall. It is situated on a gently rolling prairie, fifteen miles south of the Niobrara river, sand hills four miles south, and twelve miles west. Townsite was platted August, 1882, and now has one newspaper, two general stores, two hardware stores, two lumber yards, two land offices, two livery stables, one drug store, one restaurant, and a millinery, barber, blacksmith shop, and last of all to be mentioned, two saloons. A M. E. church is organized with a membership of thirteen.

I would take you right over this same ground, reader, after a lapse of seven months, and tell you of what I have learned of Ainsworth, and its growth since then.

Brown county was organized in March, 1883, and Ainsworth has been decided as the county seat, as it is in the centre of the populated portion of the county. But the vote is disputed, and contested by the people of Long Pine precinct, so it yet is an undecided question. Statistics of last July gave $43,000 of assessed property; eight Americans to one foreigner. I quote this to show that it is not all foreigners that go west.

"The population of Ainsworth is now 360; has three banks, and a number of business houses have been added, and a Congregational church (the result of the labor of Rev. Joseph Herbert, during his vacation months), a public building, and a $3,000 school house.

"Claims taken last spring can now be sold for from $1,000 to $1,500. A bridge has been built across the Niobrara, due north of Ainsworth. There is a a good deal of vacant government land north of the river, yet much of the best has been taken, but there are several thousand acres, good farm and grazing land, yet vacant in the county. There is a continual stream of land seekers coming in, and it is fast being taken. The sod and log 'shanties,' are fast giving way to frame dwellings, and the face of the country is beginning to assume a different appearance. Fair quality of land is selling for from three to ten dollars per acre.

"The weather has been so favorable (Dec. 11, '83) that farmers are still plowing. First frost occurred Sept. 26th. Mr. Cook, of this place, has about 8,000 head of cattle; does not provide feed or shelter for them during the winter, yet loses very few. Some look fat enough for market now, with no other feed than the prairie grass.

"School houses are now being built in nearly all the school districts. The voting population of the county at last election was 1,000. I will give you the production of the soil, and allow you to judge of its merit: Wheat from 28 to 35 bushels per acre; oats 50 to 80 bushels per acre; potatoes, weighing $3\frac{1}{2}$ pounds, and 400 bushels per acre; cabbage, 22 pounds————."

This information I received from Mr. P. D. McAndrew, who was so favorably impressed with the country, when on his visit to Fort Niobrara, that he disposed of his *Tribune* office, and returned, and took a claim near the Stone Butte, of which I have before spoken, and located at Ainsworth.

I would add that Valentine has not made much advancement, as it is of later birth, and the cow-boys still hold sway, verifying Mr. Tucker's stories as only too true by added deeds of life-taking.

You may be interested in knowing what success Rev. Herbert had in preaching in such a place. He says of the first Sabbath: "Held services in the restaurant at ten A.M., with an audience of about twenty. One saloon keeper offered to close his bar, and give me the use of the saloon for the hour. All promised to close their bars for the time, but did not. The day was very much as Saturday; if any difference the stores did a more rushing business. As far as I was privileged to meet with the cow-boys, they treated me well. They molest those only who join them in their dissipations, and yet show fear of them. No doubt there are some very low characters among them, but there is chivalry (if it may so be called) that will not brook an insult to a lady. Many of them are fugitives from justice under assumed names; others are runaways from homes in the eastern states, led to it by exciting stories of western life, found in the cheap fiction of the times, and the accounts of such men as the James boys. But there are many who remember no other life. They spend most of their time during the summer in the saddle, seldom seeing any but their companions. Their nights are spent rolled in their blankets, with the sky for their roof and sod for a pillow. They all look older than their years would warrant them in looking."

Long Pine.

After supper I walked out to see the bridge across the Long Pine creek of which I have before spoken. But I was too tired to enjoy the scenery and see it all, and concluded if the morrow was the Sabbath, there could be no harm in spending a part of it quietly seeing some of nature's grandeur, and returned to the Severance House and retired early to have a long night of rest. There is no bar connected with this hotel, although the only one in town, and a weary traveler surely rests the better for its absence.

The morning was bright and pleasant, and Mrs. H. L. Glover, of Long Pine, Mr. H. L. Hubletz, and Mr. L. A. Ross, of the colony, and myself started early for the bridge.

It is 600 feet in length, and 105 feet high. The view obtained from it is grand indeed. Looking south the narrow stream is soon lost to view by its winding course, but its way is marked by the cedar and pine trees that grow in its narrow valley, and which tower above the table-land just enough to be seen. Just above the bridge, from among the rocks that jut out of the bank high above the water, seven distinct springs gush and drip, and find their way down the bank into the stream below, mingling with the waters of the Pine and forming quite a deep pool of clear water. But like other Nebraska waters it is up and away, and with a rush and ripple glides under the bridge, around the bluffs, and far away to the north, until it kisses the waters of the Niobrara. We can follow its course north only a little way farther than we can south, but the valley and stream is wider, the bluffs higher, and the trees loftier.

It is not enough to view it at such a distance, and as height adds to grandeur more than depth, we want to get right down to the water's edge and look up at the strangely formed walls that hem them in. So we cross the bridge to the west and down the steep bank, clinging to bushes and branches to help us on our way, until we stop to drink from the springs. The water is cool and very pleasant to the taste. Then stop on a foot bridge across the pool to dip our hands in the running water, and gather a memento from its pebbly bed. On the opposite shore we view the remains of a deserted dugout and wondered who would leave so romantic a spot. Then along a well worn path that followed the stream's winding way, climbing along the bluff's edges, now pulling ourselves up by a cedar bush, and now swinging down by a grape-vine, we followed on until Mrs. G. remarked: "This is an old Indian path," which sent a cold wave over me, and looking about, half expecting to see a wandering Sioux, and not caring to meet so formidable a traveler on such a narrow pathway, I proposed that we would go no farther. So back to the bridge and beyond we went, following down the stream.

Some places the bluffs rise gradually to the table-land and are so grown with trees and bushes one can scarce tell them from Pennsylvania hills; but as a rule, they are steep, often perpendicular, from twenty-five to seventy-five feet high, forming a wall of powdered sand and clay that is so hard and compact that we could carve our initials, and many an F. F. I left to crumble away with the bluffs.

Laden with pebbles gathered from the highest points, cones from the pine trees, and flowers from the valley and sand hills, I went back from my Sabbath day's ramble with a mind full of wonder and a clear conscience. For had I not stood before preachers more powerful and no less eloquent than many who go out well versed in theology, and, too, preachers that have declaimed God's wonderful works and power ever since He spake them into existence and will ever be found at their post until the end.

But how tired we all were by the time we reached Mrs. G.'s home, where a good dinner was awaiting our whetted appetites! That over, Mr. H. stole out to Sunday School, and Mr. R. sat down to the organ. But soon a familiar chord struck home to my heart, and immediately every mile of the distance that lay between me and home came before me.

"Homesick?" Yes; so homesick I almost fainted with the first thought, but I slipped away, and offered up a prayer: my only help, but one that is all powerful in every hour and need.

Mr. Glover told us of a Mrs. Danks, living near Long Pine, who had come from Pennsylvania, and was very anxious to see some one from her native state, and Mr. Ross and I went to call on her, and found her in a large double log house on the banks of the Pine—a very pretty spot they claimed three years ago. Though ill, she was overjoyed to see us, and said:

"I heard of the colony from Pennsylvania, and told my husband I must go to see them as soon as I was able. Indeed, I felt if I could only see some one from home, it would almost cure me!"

It happened that Mr. R. knew some of her friends living in Pittsburgh, Pennsylvania, and what a treat the call was to all of us! She told us of their settling there, and how they had sheltered Crow Dog and Black Crow, when they were being taken away as prisoners. How they, and the few families living along the creek, had always held their Sabbath School and prayer meetings in their homes, and mentioned Mr. Skinner, a neighbor living not far away, who could tell us so much, as they had been living there longer, and had had more experience in pioneering. And on we went, along the creek over a half mile, to make another call.

We found Mr. and Mrs. Skinner both so kind and interesting, and their home so crowded with curiosities, which our limited time would not allow us to examine, that we yielded to their solicitaticn, and promised to spend Monday with them.

We finished the doings of our Sabbath at Long Pine by attending M. E. services at the school house, held by Rev. F. F. Thomas.

Monday—Spent the entire day at the "Pilgrim's Retreat," as the Skinner homestead is called, enjoying its romantic scenery, and best of all, Mrs. S.'s company. The house is almost hid by trees, which are leafing out, but above the tree tops, on the other side of the creek, "Dizzy Peak" towers 150 feet high from the water's edge. White Cliffs are several points, not so towering as Dizzy Peak. Hidden among these cliffs are several canyons irregular in shape and size.

Mrs. S. took me through a full suite of rooms among these canyons; and "Wild Cat gulch," 400 feet long, so named in honor of the killing of a wild cat within its walls by Adelbert Skinner, only a year ago, was explored. White Cliffs was climbed, and tired out, we sat us down in the "parlor" of the canyons, and listened to Mrs. S.'s story of her trials and triumphs. There, I know Mrs. S. will object to that word, "triumph," for she says: "God led us there to do that work, and we only did our duty."

We enjoyed listening to her story, as an earnest,

christian spirit was so plainly visible through it all, and we repeat it to show how God can and will care for his children when they call upon him.

MRS. I. S. SKINNER'S STORY.

"My husband had been in very poor health for some time, and in the spring of 1879, with the hope that he would regain not only his health, but much he had spent in doctoring, we sought a home along the Niobrara. Ignorant of the existence of the "pony-boy clan," we pitched our tent on the south side of the river, about a mile from where Morrison's bridge has since been built; had only been there a few days, when a couple of young men came, one by the name of Morrison, and the other "Doc Middleton," the noted leader of the gang of horse-thieves that surrounded us, but who was introduced as James Shepherd; who after asking Mr. S. if he was a minister, requested him to come to the little house across the river (same house where I slept on the table) and perform a marriage ceremony. On the appointed evening Mr. S. forded the river, and united him in marriage with a Miss Richards.

The room was crowded with armed men, "ready for a surprise from the Indians," they said, while the groom laid his arms off while the ceremony was being performed. Mr. S., judging the real character of the men, left as soon as his duty was performed.

About a month after this, a heavy reward was

offered for the arrest of Doc. Middleton, and two men, Llewellyn and Hazen by name, came to Middleton's tent that was hid away in a canyon, and falsely represented that they were authorized to present some papers to him, the signing of which, and leaving the country, would recall the reward. His wife strongly objected, but he, glad to so free himself —and at that time sick—signed the papers; and then was told there was one more paper to sign, and requested to ride out a short way with them.

He cheerfully mounted his pony and rode with them, but had not gone far until Hazen fell behind, and shot several times at him, badly wounding him. He in turn shot Hazen three times and left him for dead.

This happened on Sunday morning, so near our tent that we heard the shooting. Mr. S. was soon at the scene, and helped convey Hazen to our tent, after which Llewellyn fled. Middleton was taken to the "Morrison house." There the two men lay, not a mile apart. The one surrounded by a host of followers and friends, whose lives were already dark with crime and wickedness, and swearing vengeance on the betrayer of their leader, and also on anyone who would harbor or help him. The other, with only us two to stand in defiance of all their threats, and render him what aid we in our weakness could. And believing we defended a worthy man, Mr. S. declared he would protect him with his life, and would shoot anyone who would attempt to force an entrance into our tent. Fearing some would persist in coming, and knowing he would put his threats into execution if forced to it, I went to the brow of the hill and entreated those who came to turn back.

When at last Mr. Morrison said he would go, woman's strongest weapon came to my help; my tears prevailed, and he too turned back, and we were not again disturbed.

Our oldest boy, Adelbert, then 13 years old, was started to Keya Paha for a physician, and at night our three other little boys, the youngest but two years old, were tucked away in the wagon, a little way from the tent, and left in the care of the Lord, while Mr. S. and I watched the long dark night through, with guns and revolvers ready for instant action

Twice only, when we thought the man was dying, did we use a light, for fear it would make a mark at long range. We had brought a good supply of medicine with us, and knowing well its use, we administered to the man, and morning came and found him still living.

Once only did I creep out through the darkness to assure myself that our children were safe.

Monday I went to see Middleton, and carried him some medicine which he very badly needed.

After night-fall, Adelbert and the doctor came, and with them, two men, friends of Hazen, whom they met, and who inquired of the doctor of Hazen's whereabouts. The doctor after assuring himself that they were his friends, told them his mission, and brought them along, and with their help Hazen was taken away that night in a wagon; they acting as guards, the doctor as nurse, and Mr. S. as driver.

Hazen's home was in the south-east part of the state; and they took him to Columbus, then the nearest railway point. It was a great relief when they were safely started, but I was not sure they would be allowed to land in safety. Mr. S. would not be back until Thursday, and there I was, all alone with the children, my own strength nothing to depend on to defend myself against the many who felt indignant at the course we had pursued.

The nearest neighbor that we knew was truly loyal, lived fifteen miles away. Of course I knew the use of firearms, but that was not much to depend upon, and suffering from heart disease I was almost prostrated through the trouble. Threats were sent to me by the children that if Mr. S. dared to return, he would be shot down without mercy, and warning us all to leave as quickly as possible if we would save ourselves. I was helpless to do any thing but just stay and take whatever the Lord would allow to befall us. I expected every night that our cattle would be run off, and we would be robbed of everything we had. One dear old lady, who lived near, stayed a couple of nights with us, but at last told me, for the safety of her life she could not come again, and urged me to go with her to her home.

"Oh, Sister Robinson," I cried, "you *must not* leave me!" and then the thought came, how very selfish of me to ask her to risk her own life for my sake, and I told her I could stay alone.

When we were coming here, I felt the Lord was leading us, and I could not refrain from singing,

> "Through this changing world below,
> Lead me gently, gently, as I go;
> Trusting Thee. I cannot stray,
> I can never, never lose my way."

And my faith and trust did not fail me until I saw Mrs. R. going over the hill to her home, and my utter loneliness and helplessness came upon me with so much force, that I cried aloud, "Oh, Lord, why didst you lead us into all this trouble?" But a voice seemed to whisper, "Fear not; they that are for thee are more than they that are against thee." and immediately my faith and trust were not only renewed, but greatly strengthened, and I felt that I dwelt in safety even though surrounded by those who would do me harm. It was not long until Mrs. R. came back, saying she had come to stay with me, for after she got home she thought how selfish she had acted in thinking so much of her own safety, and leaving me all alone. But I assured her my fears were all dispelled, and I would not allow her to remain.

Yet I could not but feel uneasy about Mr. S., and especially as the appointed time for his return passed, and the time of anxious waiting and watching was lengthened out until the next Monday.

On Sunday a company of soldiers came and took "Doc" Middleton a prisoner. His term in the penitentiary will expire in June, and I do hope he has learned a lesson that will lead him to a better life; for he was rather a fine looking man, and is now only thirty-two years old.

(I will here add that Middleton left the penitentiary at the close of his term seemingly a reformed man, vowing to leave the West with all his bad deeds behind.)

Llewellyn received $175 for his trouble, and Hazen $250 for his death blow, for he only lived about a year after he was shot. I must say we did not approve of the way in which they attempted to take Middleton.

We did not locate there after all this happened, but went eight miles further on, to a hay ranch, and with help put up between four and five hundred tons of hay. We lived in constant watching even there, and only remained the summer, and came and homesteaded this place, which we could now sell for a good price, but we do not care to try life on the the frontier again.

In praise of the much talked-of cow-boys, I must say we never experienced any trouble from them, although many have found shelter for a night under our roof; and if they came when Mr. S. was away, they would always, without my asking, disarm themselves, and hand their revolvers to me, and ask me to lay them away until morning. This was done to assure me that I was safe at their hands.

I repeat her story word for word as nearly as possible, knowing well I repeat only truth.

And now to her collection of curiosities—but can only mention a few: One was a piece of a Mastodon's jaw-bone, found along the creek, two feet long, with teeth that would weigh about two pounds. They unearthed the perfect skeleton, but as it crumbled on exposure to the air, they left it to harden before disturbing it; and when they returned much had been carried away. The head was six feet long, and tusks, ten feet, of which they have a piece seven inches in length, fifteen inches in circumference, and weighs eight pounds, yet it was taken from near the point. Mrs. S. broke a piece off and gave to me. It is a chalky white, and shows a growth of moss like that of moss agate. She has gathered from around her home agates and moss agates and pebbles of all colors. As she handed them to me one by one, shading them from a pink topaz to a ruby, I could not help touching them to my tongue to see if they did not taste; they were so clear and rich-looking.

It seemed odd to see a chestnut burr and nut

cased as a curiosity. But what puzzled me most was a beaver's tail and paw, and we exhausted our guessing powers over it, and then had to be told. She gave it to me with numerous other things to carry home as curiosities.

There are plenty of beaver along the creek, and I could scarcely be persuaded that some naughty George Washington with his little hatchet had not felled a number of trees, and hacked around, instead of the beaver with only their four front teeth.

The timber along the creek is burr oak, black walnut, white ash, pine, cedar, hackberry, elm, ironwood, and cotton-wood. I was sorry to hear of a saw mill being in operation on the creek, sawing up quite a good deal of lumber.

Rev. Thomas makes his home with Mr. Skinner, and from him I learned he was the first minister that held services in Long Pine, which was in April, '82, in the railroad eating house, and has since held regular services every two weeks. Also preaches at Ainsworth, Johnstown, Pleasant Dale, and Brinkerhoff; only seventy of a membership in all.

Well, the pleasantest day must have an end, and after tea, a swing between the tall oak trees of their dooryard, another drink from the spring across the creek, a pleasant walk and talk with Miss Flora Kenaston, the school-mistress of Long Pine, another look at Giddy Peak and White Cliffs, and "Tramp tramp, tramp," on the organ, in which Mr. S. joined, for he was one of the Yankee soldier boys from York state, and with many thanks and promises of remembrance, I leave my newly-formed friends, carrying with me tokens of their kindness, but, best of all, fond memories of my day at "Pilgrim's Retreat."

But before I leave on the train to-night I must tell you of the beginning of Long Pine, and what it now is. The town was located in June, '81. The first train was run the following October. Mr. T. H. Glover opened the first store. Then came Mr. H. J. Severance and pitched a boarding tent, 14x16, from which they fed the workmen on the railroad, accommodating fifty to eighty men at a meal. But the tent was followed by a good hotel which was opened on Thanksgiving day. Now there is one bank, two general stores, one hardware, one grocery, one drug, and one feed store, a billiard hall, saloon, and a resturant. Population 175.

From a letter received from C. B. Glover, written December 15, I glean the following:

"You would scarcely recognize Long Pine as the little village you visited last May. There have been a good many substantial buildings put up since then. Notably is the railroad eating house, 22x86, ten two-story buildings, and many one-story. Long Pine is now the end of both passenger and freight division. The Brown County bank has moved into their 20x40 two-story building; Masonic Hall occupying the second story. The G. A. R. occupying the upper room of I. H. Skinner's hardware, where also religious services are regularly held. Preparations are being made for a good old fashioned Christmas tree. The high school, under the able managment of Rev. M. Laverty, is proving a success in every sense of the word. Mr. Ritterbush is putting in a $10,000 flouring mill on the Pine, one-half mile from town, also a saw mill at the same place. The saw mill of Mr. Upstill, on the Pine, three-fourths mile from town, has been running nearly all summer sawing pine and black walnut lumber. Crops were good, wheat going thirty bushels per acre, and corn on sod thirty. Vegetables big. A potato raised by Mr. Sheldon, near Morrison's bridge, actually measured twenty-four inches in circumference, one way, and twenty and one-half short way. It was sent to Kansas to show what the sand hills of north-western Nebraska can produce. Our government lands are fast disappearing, but by taking time, and making thorough examination of what is left, good homesteads and pre-emptions can be had by going back from the railroad ten, fifteen, and twenty miles.

"The land here is not all the same grade, a portion being fit for nothing but grazing. This is why people cannot locate at random. Timber culture relinquishments are selling for from $300 to $1,000; deeded lands from $600 to $2,000 per 160 acres. Most of this land has been taken up during the past year.

"I have made an estimate of the government land still untaken in our county, and find as follows:

"Brown county has 82 townships, 36 sections to a township, 4 quarters to a section, 11,808 quarter sections. We have about 1,500 voters. Allowing one claim to each voter, as some have two and others none, it will leave 10,308 claims standing open for entry under the homestead, pre-emption, and timber culture laws.

"Long Pine is geographically in the center of the county, and fifteen miles south of the Niobrara river. Regarding the proposed bridge across the river, it is not yet completed; think it will be this winter."

From an entirely uninterested party, and one who knows the country well, I would quote: "Should say that perhaps one-third of Brown county is too sandy for cultivation; but a great portion of it will average favorably with the states of Michigan and Indiana, and I think further developments will prove the sandhills that so many complain of, to be a good producing soil."

Water is good and easily obtained.

The lumber and trees talked of, are all in the narrow valley of the creek, and almost completely hid by its depth, so that looking around on the table-land, not a tree is to be seen. All that can be seen at a distance is the tops of the tallest trees, which look like bushes. Long Pine and Valentine are just the opposite in scenery.

The sand-hills seen about Long Pine, and all through this country, are of a clear, white sand.

But there, the train is whistling, and I must go. Though my time has been so pleasantly and profitably spent here, yet I am glad to be eastward bound.

Well, I declare! Here is Mr. McAndrew and his mother on their way back from Valentine, and also the agent, Mr. Gerdes, who says he was out on the Keya Paha yesterday (Sunday) and took a big order from a new merchant just opening a store near the colony.

Mr. McA. says they had a grand good time at the Fort, but not so pleasant was the coming from Valentine to-night, as a number of the cow boys seen at the depot Saturday morning are aboard and were drinking, playing cards, and grew quite loud over their betting. As he and his mother were the only passengers besides them, it was very unpleasant. The roughest one, he tells me, was the one I took for a ranch owner; and the most civil, the one I thought had known a better life. And there the poor boy lay, monopolizing five seats for his sole use, by turning three, and taking the cushions up from five, four to lie on, and one to prop up the back of the middle seat. It is a gift given only to cow boys to monopolize so much room, for almost anyone would sooner hang themselves to a rack, than ask that boy for a seat; so he and his companions are allowed to quietly sleep.

How glad we are to reach Stuart at last, and to be

welcomed by Mrs. Wood in the "wee sma'" hours with: "Glad you are safe back."

Stuart at the opening of 1880 was an almost untouched prairie spot, 219 miles from Missouri Valley, Iowa; but in July, 1880, Mr. John Carberry brought his family from Atkinson, and they had a "Fourth" all to themselves on their newly taken homestead, which now forms a part of the town plat, surveyed in the fall of '81; at that time having but two occupants, Carberry and Halleck. In November, the same year, the first train puffed into the new town of Stuart, so named, in honor of Peter Stuart, a Scotchman living on a homestead adjoining the town-site on the south.

Reader, do you know how an oil town is built up? Well, the building up of a town along the line of a western railroad that opens up a new, rich country, is very much the same. One by one they gather at first, until the territory is tested, then in numbers, coming from everywhere.

But the soil of Nebraska is more lasting than the hidden sea of oil of Pennsylvania, so about the only difference is that the western town is permanent. Temporary buildings are quickly erected at first, and then the substantial ones when time and money are more plenty.

So "stirring Stuart" gathered, until we now count one church (Pres.), which was used for a school room last winter, two hotels, two general stores, principal of which is Mr. John Skirving, two hardware and farm implement stores, one drug store, two lumber yards, a harness and blacksmith shop, and a bank.

Not far from Stuart, I am told, was an Indian camping ground, which was visited but two years ago by about a hundred of them, "tenting again on the old camp ground." And I doubt not but that the winding Elkhorn has here looked on wilder scenes than it did on the morning of the 27th of April, '83, when the little party of 65 colonists stepped down and out from their homes in the old "Keystone" into the "promised land," and shot at the telegraph pole, and missed it. But I will not repeat the story of the first chapter.

Now that the old year of '83 has fled since the time of which I have written, I must add what improvements, or a few at least, that the lapse of time has brought to the little town that can very appropriately be termed "the Plymouth rock of the N. M. A. C."

From The Stuart *Ledger* we quote: The Methodists have organized with a membership of twenty-four, and steps have been taken for the building of a church. Services now held every alternate Sunday by Rev. Mallory, of Keya Paha, in the Presbyterian church, of which Rev. Benson is pastor. Union Sunday school meets every Sunday, also the Band of Hope, a temperance organization. A new school house, 24x42, where over 60 children gather to be instructed by Mr. C. A. Manville and Miss Mamie Woods. An opera house 22x60, two stories high, Mrs. Arter's building, 18x24, two stories. Two M. D.'s have been added, a dentist, and a photographer. It is useless to attempt to quote all, so will close with music from the Stuart Cornet Band. From a letter received from "Sunny Side" from the pen of Mrs. W. W. Warner, Dec. 24: "Population of Stuart is now 382, an increase of 70 within the last two months. Building is still progressing, and emigrants continue to come in their 'schooners.'

"No good government land to be had near town. Soil from one to three feet deep. First frost Oct. 11. First snow, middle of November, hardly enough to speak of, and no more until 22d of December."

But to return to our story. My "Saratoga was a "traveling companion" of my own thinking up, but much more convenient, and which served as satchel and pillow. For the benefit of lady readers, I will describe its make-up. Two yards of cloth, desired width, bind ends with tape, and work corresponding eyelet holes in both ends, and put on pockets, closed with buttons, and then fold the ends to the middle of the cloth, and sew up the sides, a string to lace the ends together, and your satchel is ready to put your dress skirts, or mine at least, in full length; roll or fold the satchel, and use a shawl-strap. I did not want to be burdened and annoyed with a trunk, and improvised the above, and was really surprised at its worth as a traveling companion; so much can be carried, and smoother than if folded in a trunk or common satchel; and also used as a pillow. This with a convenient hand-satchel was all I used. These packed, and good-byes said to the remaining colonists, and the dear friends that had been friends indeed to me, and kissing "wee Nellie" last of all, I bid farewell to Stuart.

The moon had just risen to see me off. Again I am with friends. Mr. Lahaye, one of the colonists, was returning to Bradford for his family. Mrs. Peck and her daughter, Mrs. Shank, of Stuart, were also aboard.

Of Atkinson, nine miles east of Stuart, I have since gleaned the following from an old schoolmate, Rev. A. C. Spencer, of that place: "When I came to Atkinson, first of March, '83, I found two stores, two hotels, one drug store, one saloon, and three residences. Now we have a population of 300, a large school building (our schools have a nine month's session), M. E. ard Presbyterian churches, each costing about $2,000, a good grist mill, and one paper, the Atkinson *Graphic*, several stores, and many other conveniences too numerous to mention. Last March, but about fifty voters were in Atkinson precinct; now about 500. There has been a wonderful immigration to this part of Holt county during the past summer, principally from Illinois, Wisconsin, and Iowa, though quite a number from Ohio, Pennsylvania, and New York. Six miles east of this place, where not a house was to be seen the 15th of last March, is now a finely settled community, with a school house, Sunday school, and preaching every two weeks. Some good government lands can be had eight to twenty-five miles from town, but will all be taken by next May. Atkinson is near the Elkhorn river, and water is easily obtained at 20 to 40 feet. Coal is seven to ten dollars per ton."

I awoke at O'Neill just in time to see all but seven of our crowded coach get off. Some coming even from Valentine, a distance of 114 miles, to attend Robinson's circus—but shows are a rarity here. The light of a rising sun made a pleasing view of O'Neill and surrounding country: the town a little distance from the depot, gently rolling prairie, the river with its fringe of willow bushes, and here and there settlers' homes with their culture of timber.

O'Neill was founded in 1875 by Gen. O'Neill, a leader of the Fenians, and a colony of his own countrymen. It is now the county seat of Holt county, and has a population of about 800. Has three churches, Catholic, Presbyterian, and M. E.; community is largely Catholic. It has three papers, The *Frontier*, Holt County *Banner*, both republican, and O'Neill *Tribune*, Democratic, and three saloons. It is about a mile from the river. Gen. O'Neill died a few years ago in Omaha.

Neligh, the county seat of Antelope county, is situated near the Elkhorn, which is 100 to 125 feet wide, and 3 to 6 feet deep at this point. The town was platted Feb., 1873, by J. D. Neligh. Railroad was completed, and trains commenced running Aug. 29, '80. Gates college located at Neligh by the Columbus Congregational Association, Aug. '81. U. S. land office removed to Neligh in '81. M. E. church built in '83. County seat located Oct. 2, '83. Court house in course of erection, a private enterprise by the citizens.

I quote from a letter received from J. M. Coleman, and who has also given a long list of the business houses of Neligh, but it is useless to repeat, as every department of business and trade is well represented, and is all a population of 1,000 enterprising people will bring into a western town.

To write up all the towns along the way would be but to repeat much that has already been said of others, and the story of their added years of existence, that has made them what the frontier towns of to-day will be in a few years. Then why gather or glean further?

The valley of the Elkhorn is beautiful and interesting in its bright, new robes of green. At Battle Creek, near Norfolk, the grass was almost weaving high.

It was interesting to note the advance in the growth of vegetation as we went south through Madison, Stanton, Cuming and Dodge counties.

That this chapter may be complete, I would add all I know of the road to Missouri Valley—its starting point—and for this we have Mr. J. R. Buchanan for authority.

There was once a small burg called DeSoto, about five miles south of the present Blair, which was located by the S. C. & P .R. R. company in 1869, and named for the veteran, John I. Blair, of Blairstown, New Jersey, who was one of the leading spirits in the building of the road. Blair being a railroad town soon wholly absorbed DeSoto. The land was worth $1.25 per acre. To-day Blair has at least 2,500 of a population; is the prosperous county seat of Washington county. Land in the vicinity is worth from $25.00 to $40.00 per acre. The soil has no superior; this year showed on an average of twenty-five bushels of wheat per acre, and ordinarily yields sixty to eighty bushels of corn. Land up the Elkhorn Valley five years ago was $2.50 to $8.00 per acre, now it is worth from $12.00 to $30.00.

The S. C. & P. R. R. proper was built from Sioux City, Iowa, and reached Fremont, Nebraska, in 1868. It had a small land grant of only about 100,000 acres. The Fremont, Elkhorn Valley and Missouri River Railroad was organized and subsequently built from Fremont to Valentine, the direct route that nature made from the Missouri river to the Black Hills.

As to the terminus of this road, no one yet knows.

Whether, or when it will go to the Pacific coast is a question for the future. The Missouri river proper is about 2,000 feet wide. In preparing to bridge it the channel has been confined by a system of willow mattress work, until the bridge channel is covered by three spans 333 feet each or 1,000 feet. The bridge is 60 feet above water and rests on four abutments built on caissons sank to the rock fifty feet beneath the bed of the river. This bridge was completed in November, 1883, at a cost of over $1,000,000.

But good-bye, reader'; the conductor says this is Fremont, and I must leave the S. C. for the U. P. R. R. and begin a new chapter.

CHAPTER III.

Over the U. P. R. R. from North Platte to Omaha and Lincoln.
A description of the great Platte Valley.

I felt rather lonely after I had bid good-bye to my friends, but a depot is no place to stop and think, so I straightway attended to putting some unnecessary baggage in the care of the baggage-master until I returned, who said: "Just passed a resolution to-day to charge storage on baggage that is left over, but if you will allow me to remove the check, I will care for it without charge." One little act of kindness shown me already.

At the U. P. depot I introduced myself to Mr. Jay Reynolds, ticket agent, who held letters for me, and my ticket over the U. P. road, which brother had secured and left in his care. He greeted me with: "Am glad to know you are safe, Miss Fulton, your brother was disappointed at not meeting you here, and telegraphed but could get no answer. Feared you had gone to Valentine and been shot."

"Am sorry to have caused him so much uneasiness," I replied, "but the telegram came to Stuart when I was out at the location, and so could not let him hear from me, which is one of the disadvantages of colonizing on the frontier."

"Your brother said he would direct your letters in my care, and I have been inquiring for you—but you must stop on your return and see the beauties of Fremont. Mrs. Reynolds will be glad to meet you."

Well, I thought, more friends to make the way pleasant, and as it was not yet train time, I went to the post-office. The streets were thronged with people observing Decoration day. It was a real treat to see the blooming flowers and green lawns of the "Forest City;" I was almost tempted to pluck a snow-ball from a bush in the railroad garden. I certainly was carried past greener fields as the train bounded westward along the Platte valley, than I had seen north on the Elkhorn.

The Platte river is a broad, shallow stream, with low banks, and barren of everything but sand. Now we are close to its banks, and again it is lost in the distance. The valley is very wide; all the land occupied and much under cultivation.

I viewed the setting sun through the spray of a fountain in the railroad garden at Grand Island, tinging every drop of water with its amber light, making it a beautiful sight.

Grand Island is one of the prettiest places along the way, named from an island in the river forty miles long and from one to three miles wide. I was anxious to see Kearney, but darkness settled down and hindered all further sight-seeing.

The coach was crowded, and one poor old gentleman was "confidenced" out of sixty dollars, which made him almost sick, but his wife declares, "It is just good for him—no business to let the man get his hand on his money!"

"I will turn your seats for you, ladies, as soon as we have room," the conductor says; but the lady going to Cheyenne, who shares my seat, assisted, and we turn our seats without help, and I, thinking of the old gentleman's experience, lie on my pocket, and put my gloves on to protect my ring from sliding off, and sleep until two o'clock, when the conductor wakes me with, "Almost at North Platte, Miss."

I had written Miss Arta Cody to meet me, but did not know the hour would be so unreasonable. I scarcely expected to find her at the depot, but there she was standing in the chilly night air, ready to welcome me with, "I am so glad you have come, Frances)"

We had never met before, but had grown quite familiar through our letters, and it was pleasant to be received with the same familiarity and not as a stranger. We were quickly driven to her home, and found Mrs. Cody waiting to greet me.

To tell you of all the pleasures of my visit at the home of "Buffalo Bill," and of the trophies he has gathered from the hunt, chase, and trail, and seeing and hearing much that was interesting, and gleaning much of the real life of the noted western scout from

Mrs. C., whom we found to be a lady of refinement and pleasing manners, would make a long story. Their beautiful home is nicely situated one-half mile from the suburbs of North Platte. The family consists of three daughters: Arta, the eldest is a true brunette, with clear, dark complexion, black hair, perfect features, and eyes that are beyond description in color and expression, and which sparkle with the girlish life of the sweet teens. Her education has by no means been neglected, but instead is taking a thorough course in boarding school. Orra, a very pleasant but delicate child of eleven summers, with her father's finely cut features and his generous big-heartedness; and wee babe Irma, the cherished pet of all. Their only son, Kit Carson, died young.

It is not often we meet mother, daughters, and sisters so affectionate as are Mrs. C., Arta, and Orra. Mr. Cody's life is not a home life, and the mothee and daughters cling to each other, trying to fill thr void the husband and father's almost constant absence makes. He has amassed enough of this world's wealth and comfort to quietly enjoy life with his family. But a quiet life would be so contrary to the life he has always known, that it could be no enjoyment to him.

To show how from his early boyhood, he drifted into the life of the "wild west," and which has become second nature to him, I quote the following from "The Life of Buffalo Bill."

His father, Isaac Cody, was one of the original surveyors of Davenport, Iowa, and for several years drove stage between Chicago and Davenport. Was also justice of the peace, and served one term in the legislature from Iowa. Removed to Kansas in 1852, and established a trading post at Salt Creek Valley, near the Kickapoo Agency. At this time Kansas was occupied by numerous tribes of Indians who were settled on reservations, and through the territory ran the great highway to California and Salt Lake City, traveled by thousands of gold-seekers and Mormons.

Living so near the Indians, "Billy" soon became acquainted with their language, and joined them in their sport, learning to throw the lance and shoot with bow and arrow.

In 1854 his father spoke in public in favor of the Enabling Act, that had just passed, and was twice stabbed in the breast by a pro-slavery man, and by this class his life was constantly threatened; and made a burden from ill health caused by the wounds, until in '57, when he died. After the mother and children all alone had prepared the body for burial, in the loft of their log cabin at Valley Falls, a party of armed men came to take the life that had just gone out.

Billy, their only living son, was their mainstay and support, doing service as a herder, and giving his earnings to his mother. The first blood he brought was in a quarrel over a little school-girl sweet-heart, during the only term of school he ever attended, and thinking he had almost killed his little boy adversary, he fled, and took refuge in a freight wagon going to Fort Kearney, which took him from home for forty days, and then returned to find he was freely forgiven for the slight wound he had inflicted. Later he entered the employ of the great freighters, Russell, Majors & Waddell, his duty being to help with a large drove of beef cattle going to Salt Lake City to supply Gen. A. S. Johnson's army, then operating against the Mormons, who at that time were so bitter that they employed the help of the Indians to massacre over-land freighters and emigrants. The great freighting business of this firm was done in wagons carrying a capacity of 7,000 pounds, and drawn by from eight to ten teams of oxen. A train consisted of twenty-five wagons. We must remember this was before a railroad spanned the continent, and was the only means of transportation beyond the states.

It was on his first trip as freight boy that Billy Cody killed his first Indian. When just beyond old Ft. Kearney they were surprised by a party of Indians, and the three night herders while rounding up the cattle, were killed. The rest of the party retreated after killing several braves, amd when near Plum Creek, Billy became separated from the rest, and seeing an Indian peering at him over the bluffs of the creek, took aim and brought to the dust his first Indian. This "first shot" won for him a name and notoriety enjoyed by none nearly so young as he, and filled him with ambition and daring for the life he has since led. Progressing from freight boy to pony express rider, stage driver, hunter, trapper, and Indian scout in behalf of the government, which office he filled well and was one of the best, if not the very best, scouts of the plains; was married in March, '65, to Miss Louisa Fredrica, of French descent, of St. Louis; was elected to legislature in 1871, but the place was filled by another while he continued his exhibitions on the stage.

When any one is at loss for a name for anything they wish to speak of, they just call it buffalo——and as a consequence, there are buffalo gnats, buffalo birds, buffalo fish, buffalo beans, peas, berries, moss, grass, burrs, and "Buffalo Bill," a title given to William Cody, when he furnished buffalo meat for the U. P. R. R. builders and hunted with the Grand Duke Alexis, and has killed as high as sixty-nine in one day.

I did not at the time of visiting North Platte think of writing up the country so generally, so did not make extra exertions to see and learn of the country as I should have done. And as there was a shower almost every afternoon of my stay, we did not get to drive out as Miss Arta and I had planned to do. North Platte, the county-seat of Lincoln county, is located 291 miles west of Omaha, and is 2,789 feet above the sea level, between and near the junction of the North and South Platte rivers. The U. P. R. R. was finished to this point first of December, 1866, and at Christmas time there were twenty buildings erected on the town site. Before the advent of the railroad, when all provisions had to be freighted, one poor meal cost from one to two dollars.

North Platte is now nicely built up with good homes and business houses, and rapidly improving in every way. The United States Land office of the western district embraces the government land of Cheyenne, Keith, Lincoln, a part of Dawson, Frontier, Gosper, and Custer counties and all unorganized territory. All I can see of the surrounding country is very level and is used for grazing land, as stock raising is the principal occupation of the people. Alkali is quite visible on the surface, but Mrs. C. says both it and the sand are fast disappearing, and the rainfall increasing. No trees to be seen but those which have been cultivated.

Mrs. C. in speaking of the insatiable appetite and stealthy habits of the Indians, told of a dinner she had prepared at a great expense and painstaking for six officers of Ft. McPherson, whom Mr. C. had invited to share with him, and while she was receiving them at the front door six Indians entered at a rear door, surrounded the table, and without ceremony or carving knife, were devouring her nicely roasted chickens and highly enjoying the good things they had found when they were discovered, which was not until she led the way to the dining room, thinking with so much pride of the delicacies she had prepared, and how they would enjoy it.

"Well, the dinner was completely spoiled by the six uninvited guests, but while I cried with mortification, the officers laughed and enjoyed the joke."

Ft. McPherson was located eighteen miles east of North Platte, but was abandoned four years ago.

Notwithstanding their kindness and entertaining home I was anxious to be on the home way, and biding Mrs. C. and Arta good-bye at the depot, I left Monday evening for Plum Creek.

How little I thought when I kissed the dear child Orra good-bye, and whom I had already learned to love, that I would have the sad duty of adding a tribute to her memory. Together we took my last walk about their home, gathering pebbles from their gravel walks, flowers from the lawn and leaves from the trees, for me to carry away.

I left her a very happy child over the anticipation of a trip to the east where the family would join Mr. Cody for some time. I cannot do better than to quote from a letter received from the sorrow-stricken mother.

"Orra, my precious darling, that promised so fair, was called from us on the 24th of October, '83, and we carried her remains to Rochester, N. Y., and laid them by the side of her little brother, in a grave lined with evergreens and flowers. When we visited the sacred spot last summer, she said: 'Mamma, won't you lay me by brother's side when I die?' Oh, how soon we have had to grant her request! If it was not for the hope of heaven and again meeting there, my affliction would be more than I could bear, but I have consigned her to Him who gave my lovely child to me for these short years, and can say, 'Thy will be done.'"

Night traveling again debarred our seeing much that would have been interesting, but it was my most convenient train, and an elderly lady from Ft. Collins, Colorado, made the way pleasant by telling of how they had gone to Colorado from Iowa, four years ago, and now could not be induced to return. Lived at the foot of mountains that had never been without a snow-cap since she first saw them.

Arrived at Plum Creek about ten o'clock, and as I had no friends to meet me here, asked to be directed to a hotel, and remarked that we preferred a temperance hotel. "That's all the kind we keep here," the gentleman replied with an injured air, and I was shown to the Johnston House.

I had written to old friends and neighbors who had left Pennsylvania about a year ago, and located twenty-five miles south-west of Plum creek, to meet me here; but letters do not find their way out to the little sod post-offices very promptly, and as I waited their coming Tuesday, I spent the day in gathering of the early history of Plum Creek.

Through the kindness of Mrs. E. D. Johnston, we were introduced to Judge R. B. Pierce, who came from Maryland to Plum Creek, in April, 1873, and was soon after elected county judge, which office he still holds. He told how they had found no signs of a town but a station house, and lived in box-cars with a family of five children until he built a house, which was the first dwelling-house on the present town-site. One Daniel Freeman had located and platted a town-site one mile east, but the railroad company located the station just a mile further west.

Judge Pierce gave me a supplement of the Dawson County *Pioneer*, of date July 20th, 1876, from which I gather the following history:

"On June 26th, 1871, Gov. W. H. James issued a proclamation for the organization of the county. At the first election, held July 11, '71, at the store of D. Freeman, there were but thirteen votes cast, and the entire population of the county did not exceed forty souls, all told. But the Centennial Fourth found a population of 2,716 prosperous people, 614 of whom are residents of Plum Creek, which was incorporated March, 1874, and named for a creek a few miles east tributary to the Platte; and which in old staging days was an important point.

"The creek rises in a bluffy region and flows north-east, the bluffs affording good hiding places for the stealthy Indians.

"Among the improvements of the time is a bridge spanning the Platte river, three miles south of the town, the completion of which was celebrated July 4th, '73, and was the first river bridge west of Columbus.

"In '74 the court house was built. We will quote in full of the churches, to show that those who go west do not always leave their religion behind. As early as 1867, the Rev. Father Ryan, of the Catholic church, held services at the old station house. In the fall of '72, Rev. W. Wilson organized the first Methodist society in the county, with a membership of about thirty. In April, '74, Right Rev. Bishop Clarkson organized Plum Creek parish, and a church was built in '75, which was the first church built in the town. In '74 the Missionary Baptist Society was formed. In '73 the Presbyterian congregation was organized by Rev. S. M. Robinson, state missionary.

"Settlements in Plum Creek precinct were like angels' visits, few and far between, until April 9th, 1872, when the Philadelphia Nebraska colony arrived, having left Philadelphia, Pennsylvania, April 2d, under charge of F. J. Pearson.

"In this colony there were sixty-five men, women, and children. Their first habitation was four box-cars, kindly placed on a side track by the U. P. R. R. Co. for their use until they could build their houses."

I met one of these colonists, B. F. Krier, editor *Pioneer*, whom I questioned as to their prosperity. He said: "Those who remained have done well, but some returned, and others have wandered farther west, until there is not many of us left; only about eight families that are now residents of the town. We were so completely eaten out by the grasshoppers in '73–74, and in 78 there was a drought, and it was very discouraging."

I thought of the sixty-five colonists who had just landed and drove their stakes in the soil of northern Nebraska, and hoped they may be driven deep and firm, and their trials be less severe.

"The Union Pacific windmill was their only guide to lead them over the treeless, stoneless, trackless prairie, and served the purpose of light-house to many a prairie-bewildered traveler. A few days after they landed, they had an Indian scare. But the seven Sioux, whose mission was supposed to be that of looking after horses to steal, seeing they were prepared for them, turned and rode off. Six miles west of Plum Creek in 1867, the Indians wrecked a freight train, in which two men were killed, and two escaped; one minus a scalp, but still living."

Mrs. E. D. Johnston told of how they came in 1878, and opened a hotel in a 16x20 shanty, with a sod kitchen attached; and how the cattle men, who were their principal stoppers, slept on boxes and in any way they could, while they enlarged their hotel at different times until it is now the Johnston House, the largets and best hotel in Plum Creek.

While interviewing Judge Pierce, a man entered the office, to transact some business, and as he left, the Judge remarked—

"That man came to me to be married about a year ago, and I asked him how old the lady was he wished to marry. 'Just fifteen,' he answered. I can't grant you a license, then; you will have to wait a year. 'Wait?' ¦No; he got a buggy, drove post-haste down into Kansas, and was married. He lives near your friends, and if you wish I will see if he can take you out with him." So, through his help, I took passage in Mr. John Anderson's wagon, Wednesday noon, along with his young wife, and a family just from Luzerne county, Pennsylvania.

The wind was strong and the sun warm, but I was eager to improve even this opportunity to get to my friends.

Going south-east from Plum Creek, we pass over land that is quite white with alkali, but beyond the river there is little surface indication of it. For the novelty of crossing the Platte river on foot, I walked the bridge, one mile in length, and when almost across met Mr. Joseph Butterbaugh—our old neighbor—coming to town, and who was greatly surprised, as they had not received my letter.

We had not gone far until our faces were burning with the hot wind and sun, and for a protection we tied our handkerchiefs across our faces, just below our eyes. The load was heavy, and we went slowly west along the green valley, the river away to our right, and a range of bluffs to our left, which increase in height as we go westward. Passed finely improved homes that had been taken by the first settlers, and others where the new beginners yet lived in their "brown stone fronts" (sod houses).

Four years ago this valley was occupied by Texas cattle, 3,000 in one herd, making it dangerous for travelers.

Stopped for a drink at a large and very neat story and a-half sod house built with an L; shingled roof, and walls as smooth and white as any lathed and plastered walls, and can be papered as well. Sod houses are built right on the top of the ground, without the digging or building of a foundation. The sod is plowed and cut the desired size, and then built the same as brick, placing the grassy side down. The heat of the summer can hardly penetrate the thick walls, and, too, they prove a good protection from the cold winds of winter. Sod corrals are used for sheep.

Almost every family have their "western post-office:" a little box nailed to a post near the road, where the mail carrier deposits and receives the mail.

Now for many miles west the government land is taken, and the railroad land bought. Much of the land is cultivated and the rest used for pasture. The corn is just peeping through the sod.

Passed two school houses, one a sod, and the other an 8x10 frame, where the teacher received twenty-five dollars per month. It is also used for holding preaching, Sunday School, and society meetings in.

It is twenty miles to Mr. Anderson's home, and it is now dark; but the stars creep out from the ether blue, and the new moon looks down upon us lonely travelers. "Oh, moon, before you have waned, may I be safe in my own native land!" I wished, when I first saw its golden crest. I know dear mother will be wishing the same for me, and involuntarily sang:

"I gaze on the moon as I tread the drear wild,
And feel that my mother now thinks of her child,
As she looks on that moon from our own cottage door,
Thro' the woodbine whose fragrance shall cheer me some more."

I could not say "no more." To chase sadness away I sang, and was joined by Mr. A., who was familiar with the songs of the old "Key Note," and together we sang many of the dear old familiar pieces. But none could I sing with more emphasis than—

"Oh give me back my native hills,
Rough, rugged though they be,
No other land, no other clime
Is half so dear to me."

But I struck the key note of his heart when I sang, "There's a light in the window for thee," in which he joined at first, but stopped, saying:

"I can't sing that; 'twas the last song I sung with my brothers and sisters the night before I left my Kentucky home, nine years ago, and I don't think I have tried to sing it since."

All along the valley faint lights glimmered from lonely little homes. I thought every cottager should have an Alpine horn, and as the sun goes down, a "good night" shouted from east to west along the valley, until it echoed from bluff to bluff.

But the longest journey must have an end, and at last we halted at Mr. A.'s door, too late for me to go farther. But was off early in the morning on horseback, with Zeke Butterbaugh, who was herding for Mr. A., to take his mother by surprise, and breakfast with her.

Well, reader, I would not ask anyone, even my worst enemy, to go with me on that morning ride.

Rough?

There now, don't say anything more about it. It is good to forget some things; I can feel the top of my head flying off yet with every jolt, as that horse *tried* to trot—perhaps it was my poke hat that was coming off. If the poor animal had had a shoe on, I would have quoted Mark Twain, hung my hat on its ear and looked for a nail in its foot.

When we reached Mrs. B.'s home, we found it deserted, and we had to go three miles farther on. Six miles before breakfast.

"Now,"Zeke, we will go direct; take straight across

and I will follow: mind, we don't want to be going round many corners."

"Well, watch, or your horse will tramp in a gopher hole and throw you; can you stand another trot?"

And I would switch my trotter, but would soon have to rein him up, and laugh at my attempt at riding.

It was not long until we were within sight of the house where Zeke's sister lived, and when within hearing distance we ordered—"Breakfast for two!" When near the house we concentrated all our equestrian skill into a "grand gallop."

Mrs. B. and Lydia were watching and wondering who was coming; but my laugh betrayed me, and when we drew reins on our noble ponies at the door, I was received with: "I just knew that was Pet Fulton by the laugh;" and as I slipped down, right into their arms, I thought after all the ride was well worth the taking, and the morning a grand one. Rising before the sun, I watched its coming, and the mirage on the river, showing distinctly the river, islands, and towns; but all faded away as the mirage died out, and then the ride over the green prairie, bright with flowers, and at eight o'clock breakfasting with old friends.

We swung around the circle of Indiana county friends, the Butterbaughs and Fairbanks, until Monday. Must say I enjoyed the *swing* very much.

Took a long ramble over the bluffs that range east and west, a half mile south of Mr. J. B.'s home. Climbed bluff after bluff, only to come to a jumping off place of from 50 to 100 feet straight down. To peer over these places required a good deal of nerve, but I held tight to the grass or a soap weed stalk, and looked. We climbed to the top of one of the highest, from which we could see across the valley to the Platte river three miles away—the river a mile in width, and the wide valley beyond, to the bluffs that range along its northern bounds. The U. P. R. R. runs on the north side of the river, and Mr. B. says the trains can be seen for forty miles. Plum Creek, twenty miles to the east, is in plain view, the buildings quite distinguishable. Then comes Cozad, Willow Island—almost opposite, and Gothenburg, where the first house was built last February, and now has about twenty. I would add the following from a letter received Dec. 21, '83:

Gothenburg has now 40 good buildings, and in the county where but five families lived in the spring of '82, now are 300, and that number is to be more than doubled by spring.

But to the bluffs again. To the south, east, and west, it is wave after wave of bluffs covered with buffalo grass; not a tree or bush in sight until we get down into the canyons, which wind around among the hills and bluffs like a grassy stream, without a drop of water, stone or pebble; now it is only a brook in width, now a creek, and almost a river. The pockets that line the canyons are like great chambers, and are of every size, shape and height. A clay like soil they call calcine, in strata from white to reddish brown, forms their walls. They seemed like excellent homes for wild cats, and as we were only armed with a sunflower stalk which we used for a staff (how æsthetic we have grown since coming west!) we did not care to prospect—would much rather look at the deer tracks.

The timber in the canyons are ash, elm, hackberry, box elder, and cottonwood, but Mr. B. has to go fifteen miles for wood as it is all taken near him. Wild plums, choke cherries, currants, mountain cranberries, and snow berries grow in wild profusion, and are overrun with grape-vines.

Found a very pretty pincushion cactus in bloom, and I thought to bring it home to transplant; but cactus are not "fine" for bouquets nor fragrant; and if they were, who would risk a smell at a cactus flower? But I did think I would like a prairie dog for a pet, and a full grown doggie was caught and boxed for me. Had a great mind to attempt bringing a jack rabbit also, and open up a Nebraska menagerie when I returned. Jack rabbits are larger than the common rabbits and very deceitful, and if shot at will pretend they are hurt, even if not touched. A hunter from the east shot at one, and seeing it hop off so lame, threw down his gun and ran to catch it—

well, he didn't catch the rabbit, and spent two days in searching before he found his gun.

Sunday. We attended Sabbath school in the sod school house, and Monday morning early were off on the long ride back to Plum creek with Mr. and Mrs. H. Fairbanks and Miss Laura F. We picnicked at dinner time. Under a shade tree? No, indeed; not a tree to be seen—only a few willows on the islands in the river, showing that where it is protected from fires, timber will grow. But in a few years this valley will be a garden of cultivated timber and fields. I must speak of the brightest flower that is blooming on it now; 'tis the buffalo pea, with blossoms same as our flowering pea, in shape, color, and fragrance, but it is not a climber. How could it be, unless it twined round a grass stalk?

The Platte valley is from six to fifteen miles wide, but much the widest part of the valley is north of the river. The bluffs on the north are rolling, and on the south abrupt. In the little stretch of the valley that I have seen, there is no sand worthy of notice. Water is obtained at from twenty to fifty feet on the valley, but on the table-land at a much greater depth. Before we reached the bridge, we heard it was broken down, and no one could cross. "Cannot we ford it?" I asked. "No, the quicksand makes it dangerous." "Can we cross on a boat, then?" "A boat would soon stick on a sand bar. No way of crossing if the bridge is down." But we found the bridge so tied together that pedestrians could cross. As I stooped to dip my hand in the muddy waves of the Platte I thought it was little to be admired but for its width, and the few green islands. The banks are low, and destitute of everything but grass.

The Platte river is about 1,200 miles long. It is formed by the uniting of the South Platte that rises in Colorado, and the North Platte that rises in Wyoming. Running east through Nebraska, it divides into the North and South Platte. About two-thirds of the state being on the north. It finds an outlet in the Missouri river at Plattsmouth, Neb. It has a fall of about 5 feet to the mile, and is broad, shallow, and rapid—running over a great bed of sand that is constantly washing and changing, and so mingled with the waters that it robs it of its brightness. Its shallowness is thought to be owing to a system of under ground drainage through a bed of sand, and supplies the Republican river in the southern part of the state, which is 352 feet lower than the Platte.

We were fortunate in securing a hack for the remaining three miles of our journey, and ten o'clock found me waiting for the eastern bound train. I would add that Plum Creek now has a population of 600. I have described Dawson county more fully as it was in Central Nebraska our colony first thought of locating, and a number of them have bought large tracts of land in the south-western part of the county. That the Platte valley is very fertile is beyond a doubt. It is useless to give depth of soil and its production, but will add the following:

Mr. Joseph Butterbaugh reports for his harvest of 1883, 778 bushels wheat from 35 acres. Corn averaged 35 bushels, shelled; oats 25 to 30; and barley about 40 bushels per acre.

First frost was on the 9th of October. Winter generally begins last of December, and ends with February. The hottest day of last summer was 108 degrees in the shade. January 1, 1884, it was 8 degrees below, which is the lowest it has yet (January 15) fallen, and has been as high as 36 above since.

The next point of interest on the road is Kearney, where the B. & M. R. R. forms a junction with the U. P. R. R.

In looking over the early history of Buffalo county we find it much the same, except in dates a little earlier than that of Dawson county. First settlers in the county were Mormons, in 1858, but all left in '63. The county was not organized until in '70, and the first tax list shows but thirty-eight names. Kearney, the county-seat, is on the north side of the river 200 miles west and little south of Omaha, and 160 miles west of Lincoln. Lots in Kearney was first offered for sale in '72, but the town was not properly organized until in '73. Since that time its growth has been rapid; building on a solid foundation and bringing its churches and schools with it, and now has under good way a canal to utilize the waters of the Platte.

Fremont the "Forest City," is truly so named from the many trees that hide much of the city from view, large heavy bodied trees of poplar, maple, box-elder, and many others that have been cultivated. Fremont, named in honor of General Fremont and his great overland tour in 1842 and, was platted in 1855 on lands which the Pawnee Indians had claimed but which had been bought from them, receiving $20,000 in gold and silver and $20,000 in goods. In '56 Mr. S. Turner swam the Platte river and towed the logs across that built the old stage house which his mother Mrs. Margaret Turner kept, but which has given way to the large and commodious "New York Hotel." The 4th of July, '56, was celebrated at Fremont by about one hundred whites and a multitude of Indians; but now it can boast of over 5,000 inhabitants, fine schools and churches. It is the junction of the U. P. R. R. and the S. C. & P. R. R. I must add that it was the only place of all that I visited where I found any sickness, and that was on the decrease, but diphtheria had been bad for some time, owing, some thought, to the use of water obtained too near the surface, and the many shade trees, as some of the houses are entirely obscured from the direct rays of the sun.

I will not attempt to touch on the country as we

neared Omaha along the way, as it is all improved lands, and I do not like its appearance as well as much of the unimproved land I have seen. We reached Omaha about seven o'clock. I took a carriage for the Millard hotel and had breakfast. At the request of my brother I called on Mr. Leavitt Burnham, who has held the office of Land Commissioner of the U. P. R. R. land company since 1878, and fills it honestly and well.

Omaha, the "Grand Gateway of the West," was named for the Omaha Indians, who were the original landholders, but with whom a treaty was made in 1853. William D. Brown, who for two or three years had been ferrying the "Pike's Peak or bust" gold hunters from Iowa to Nebraska shores, and "busted" from Nebraska to Iowa, in disgust entered the present site of Omaha, then known as the Lone Tree Ferry, as a homestead in the same year. In the next year the city of Omaha was founded. The "General Marion" was the first ferry steamer that plied across the Missouri at this point, for not until in '68 was the bridge completed. All honor to the name of Harrison Johnston, who plowed the first furrow of which there is any record, paying the Indians ten dollars for the permit. He also built the first frame house in Omaha, and which is yet standing near the old Capitol on Capitol Hill.

The first religious services held in Omaha were under an arbor erected for the first celebration of the

Fourth of July, by Rev. I. Heaton, Congregationalist. Council Bluffs, just opposite Omaha, on the Iowa shore, was, in the early days, used as a "camping ground" by the Mormons, where they gathered until a sufficient number was ready to make a train and take up the line of march over the then great barren plains of Nebraska. Omaha is situated on a plateau, over fifty feet above the river, which is navigable for steamers only at high water tides. It is 500 miles from Chicago, and 280 miles north of St. Louis. It was the capital of Nebraska until it was made a state. What Omaha now is would be vain for me to attempt to tell. That it is Nebraska's principal city, with 40,000 inhabitants, is all-sufficient.

I had written my friends living near Lincoln to meet me on Monday, and as this was Tuesday there was no one to meet me when I reached Lincoln, about four o'clock. Giving my baggage in charge of the baggage-master, and asking him to take good care of my doggie, I asked to be directed to a hotel, and left word where my friends would find me. The Arlington House was crowded, and then I grew determined to in some way reach my friends. Had I known where they lived I could have employed a liveryman to take me to them. I knew they lived four miles west of Lincoln, and that was all. Well, I thought, there cannot be many homœopathic physicians in Lincoln, and one of them will surely know where Gardners live, for their doctor was often called when living in Pennsylvania. But a better thought came—that of the Baptist minister, as they attended that church. I told the clerk at the hotel my dilemma, and through his kindness I learned where the minister lived, whom, after a long walk, I found. "I am sorry I have no way of taking you to your friends, but as it is late we would be glad to have you stop with us to-night, and we will find a way to-morrow." I thankfully declined his kind offer, and he then directed me to Deacon Keefer's, where Cousin Gertrude made her home while attending school. After another rather long walk, tired and bewildered, I made inquiry of a gentleman I met. "Keefer? Do they keep a boarding-house?" "I believe so." "Ah, well, if you will follow me I will show you right to the house." Another mile walk, and it wasn't the right Keefer's; but they searched the City Directory, and found that I had to more than retrace my steps. "Since I have taken you so far out of your way, Miss, I will help you to find the right place," and at last swung open the right gate; and as I stood waiting an answer to my ring, I thought I had seen about all of Lincoln in my walking up and down—at least all I cared to. But the welcome "Trude's Cousin Pet" received from the Keefer family, added to the kindness others had shown me, robbed my discomfiture of much of its unpleasantness. Soon another plate was added to the tea-table, and I was seated drinking iced-tea and eating strawberries from their own garden, as though I was an old friend, instead of a straggling stranger. Through it all I learned a lesson of kindness that nothing but experience could have taught me. After tea Mr. Ed. and Miss Marcia Keefer drove me out to my friends, and as I told them how I thought of finding them through the doctors, Cousin Maggie said: "Well, my girlie, you would have failed in that, for in the four years we have lived in Nebraska we have never had to employ a doctor."

And, reader, now "let's take a rest," but wish to add before closing this chapter, that the U. P. R. R. was the first road built in Nebraska. Ground was broken at Omaha, December 2, 1863, but '65 found only forty miles of track laid. The road reached Julesburg, now Denver Junction, in June, '67, and the "golden spike" driven May 10, 1869, which connected the Union Pacific with the Central Pacific railroad, and was the first railroad that spanned the continent. The present mileage is 4,652 miles, and several hundred miles is in course of construction. J. W. Morse, of Omaha, is general passenger agent. The lands the company yet have for sale are in Custer, Lincoln, and Cheyenne counties, where some government land is yet to be had.

A colony, known as the "Ex-Soldiers' Colony," was formed in Lincoln, Nebraska, in 1883. It accepted members from everywhere, and now April 24, '84, shows a roll of over two hundred members, many of whom have gone to the location, forty miles north-east of North Platte, in unorganized territory, and near the Loup river. Six hundred and forty acres were platted into a town site in spring of '84, and named Logan, in honor of Gen. John A. Logan. Quite a number are already occupying their town lots, and building permanent homes, and most of the land within reach has been claimed by the colonists. The land is all government land, of which about one-half is good farming land, and rest fit only for grazing.

This is only one of the many colonies that have been planted on Nebraska soil thus early in '84, but is one that will be watched with much interest, composed as it is of the good old " boys in blue."

CHAPTER IV.

Over the B. & M. R. R. from Lincoln to McCook, via Wymore, and return via Hastings.—A description of the Republican and Blue Valleys.—The Saratoga of Nebraska.

We rested just one delightful week, talking the old days over, making point lace, stealing the first ripe cherries, and pulling grass for "Danger"—danger of it biting me or getting away—my prairie dog, which had found a home in a barrel.

One evening Cousin Andy said:

"I'll give you twenty-five cents for your dog, Pet?"

"Now, Cousin, don't insult the poor dog by such a price. They say they make nice pets, and I am going to take my dog home for Norval. But that reminds me I must give it some fresh grass," and away I went, gathering the tenderest, but, alas! the barrel was empty, and a hole gnawed in the side told the story.

I wanted to sell the dog then, and would have taken almost any price for the naughty Danger, that, though full grown, was no bigger than a Norway rat; but no one seemed to want to buy him.

The weather was very warm, but poor "Wiggins" was left on the parlor table in the hotel at Plum Creek one night, and in the morning I found him scalped, and all his prophetic powers destroyed, so we did not know just when to look out for a storm, but thunder storms, accompanied with heavy rains, came frequently during the week, generally at night, but by morning the ground would be in good working order.

Our cousin, A. M. Gardner, formerly of Franklin, Pennsylvania, for several years was one of the fortunate oil men of the Venango county field, but a couple of years of adverse fortunes swept all, and leaving their beautiful home on Gardner's Hill, came west, and are now earnestly at work building upon a surer foundation.

When I was ready to be off for Wymore, Tuesday, Salt Creek Valley was entirely covered with water, and even the high built road was so completely hidden that the drive over it was dangerous, but Cousin Rob Wilhelm took me as far as a horse could go, and thanks to a high-built railroad and my light luggage, we were able to walk the rest of the way. The overflow of Salt Creek Valley is not an uncommon occurrence in the spring of the year. This basin or valley covers about 500 acres, and is rather a barren looking spot. In dry weather the salt gathers until the ground is quite white, and before the days of railroads, settlers gathered salt for their cattle from this valley. The water has an ebb and flow, being highest in the morning and lowest in afternoon.

I had been directed to call upon Mr. R. R. Randall, immigration agent of the B. & M. R. R., for information about southern Nebraska, and while I waited for the train, I called upon him in his office, on the third floor of the depot, and told him I had seen northern and central Nebraska, and was anxious to know all I could of southern Nebraska.

After a few moments conversation, he asked:

"What part of Pennsylvania are you from, Miss Fulton?"

"Indiana county."

"Indeed? why, I have been there to visit a good old auntie; but she is dead now, bless her dear soul," and straightway set about showing me all kindness and interest.

At first I flattered myself that it was good to hail from the home of his "good old auntie," but I soon learned that I only received the same kindness and attention that every one does at his hands.

"Now, Miss Fulton, I would like you to see all you can of southern Nebraska, and just tell the plain truth about it. For, remember, that truth is the great factor that leads to wealth and happiness;" then seeing me safe aboard the train, I was on my way to see more friends and more of the state.

A young lady, who was a cripple, shared her seat with me, but her face was so mild and sweet I soon forgot the crutch at her side. She told me she was called home by the sudden illness of a brother, who was not expected to live, and whom she had not seen since in January last.

Poor girl! I could truly sympathize with her through my own experience: I parted with a darling sister on her fifteenth birthday, and three months after her lifeless form was brought home to me without one word of warning, and I fully realized what it would be to receive word of my young brother, whom I had not seen since in January, being seriously ill. When her station was reached, the brakeman very kindly helped her off and my pleasant company was gone with my most earnest wishes that she might find her brother better.

The sun was very bright and warm, and to watch the country hurt my eyes, so I gave my attention to the passengers. Before me sat a perfect snapper of a miss, so cross looking, and just the reverse in expression from her who had sat with me. Another lady was very richly dressed, but that was her most attractive feature; yet she was shown much attention by a number. Another was a mother with two sweet children, but so cold and dignified, I wondered she did not freeze the love of her little ones. Such people are as good as an arctic wave, and I enjoy them just as much. In the rear of the coach were a party of emigrants that look as though they had just crossed the briny wave. They are the first foreigners I have yet met with in the cars, and they go to join a settlement of their own countrymen. Foreigners locate as closely together as possible.

I was just beginning to grow lonely when an elderly gentlemen whom I had noticed looking at me quite earnestly, came to me and asked:

"Are you not going to Wymore, Miss?"

"Yes, sir."

"To Mr. Fulton's?"

"Why, yes. You know my friends then?"

"Yes, and it was your resemblance to one of the girls, that I knew where you were going."

No one had ever before told me that I favored this cousin in looks, but then there are just as many different eyes in this world as there are different people.

"I met Miss Emma at the depot a few days ago, and she was disappointed at the non-arrival of a cousin, and I knew at first glance that you was the one she had expected."

"You know where they live then?"

"Yes, and if there is no one at the train to meet you, I will see you to the house."

With this kind offer, Mr. Burch, one of Wymore's bankers went back to his seat. As I had supposed, my friends had grown tired meeting me when I didn't come, as I had written to them I would be there the previous week. But Mr. Burch kindly took one of my satchels, and left me at my Uncle's door.

"Bless me! here is Pet at last!" and dear Aunt Jane's arms are around me, and scolding me for disappointing them so often.

"The girls and Ed. have been to the depot so often, and I wanted them to go to-day, but they said they just knew you would'nt come. I thought you would surely be here to eat your birthday dinner with us yesterday."

"Well, Auntie, Salt Valley was overflooded, and I could'nt get to the depot; so I ate it with cousin Maggie. But that is the way; I come just when I am given up for good."

Then came Uncle John, Emma, Annie, Mary, Ed, and Dorsie, with his motherless little Gracie and Arthur. After the first greeting was over, Aunt said:

"What a blessing it is that Norval got well!"

"Norval got well? Why Aunt, what do you mean?"

"Didn't they write to you about his being so sick?"

"No, not a word."

"Well, he was very low with scarlet fever, but he is able to be about now."

"Oh! how thankful I am! What if Norval had died, and I away!" And then I told of the lady I had met that was going to see her brother, perhaps already dead, and how it had brought with such force the thought of what such word would be to me about Norval. How little we know what God in His great loving kindness is sparing us!

I cannot tell you all the pleasure of this visit. To be at "Uncle John's" was like being at home; for we had always lived in the same village and on adjoining farms. Then too, we all had the story of the year to tell since they had left Pennsylvania for Nebraska. But the saddest story of all was the death of Dorsie's wife, Mary Jane, and baby Ruth, with malaria fever.

To tell you of this country, allow me to begin with Blue Springs—a town just one mile east, on the line of the U. P. R. R., and on the banks of the Big Blue river, which is a beautiful stream of great volume, and banks thickly wooded with heavy timber —honey locust, elm, box elder, burr oak, cottonwood, hickory, and black walnut. The trees and bushes grow down into the very water's edge, and dip their branches in its waves of blue. This river rises in Hamilton county, Nebraska, and joins the Republican river in Kansas. Is about 132 miles long.

I cannot do better than to give you Mr. Tyler's story as he gave it to us. He is a hale, hearty man of 82 years, yet looks scarce 70; and just as genteel in his bearing as though his lot had ever been cast among the cultured of our eastern cities, instead of among the early settlers of Nebraska, as well as with the soldiers of the Mexican war. He says:

"In 1859 I was going to join Johnston's army in Utah, but I landed in this place with only fifty cents in my pocket, and went to work for J. H. Johnston, who had taken the first claim when the county was first surveyed and organized. About the only settlers here at that time were Jacob Poof, M. Stere, and Henry and Bill Elliott, for whom Bill creek is named. The houses were built of unhewn logs.

"Soon after I came there was talk of a rich widow that was coming among us, and sure enough she did come, and bought the first house that had been built in Blue Springs (it was a double log house), and opened the first store. But we yet had to go to Brownville, 45 miles away, on the Missouri river for many things, as the 'rich widow's' capital was only three hundred dollars. Yet, that was a great sum to pioneer settlers. Indeed, it was few groceries we used; I have often made pies out of flour and water and green grapes without any sugar; and we thought them quite a treat. But we used a good deal of corn, which was ground in a sheet-iron mill that would hold about two quarts, and which was nailed to a post for everybody to use.

"Well, we thought we must have a Fourth of July that year, and for two months before, we told every one that passed this way to come, and tell everybody else to come. And come they did—walking, riding in ox wagons, and any way at all—until in all there was 150 of us. The ladies in sunbonnets and very plain dresses; there was one silk dress in the crowd, and some of the men shoeless. Everyone brought all the dishes they had along, and we had quite a dinner on fried fish and corn dodgers. For three days before, men had been fishing and grinding corn.

The river was full of catfish which weighed from 6 to 80 pounds. We sent to Brownville, and bought a fat pig to fry our fish and dodgers with. A Mr. Garber read the Declaration of Independence, we sang some war songs, and ended with a dance that lasted until broad daylight. Very little whiskey was used, and there was no disturbance of any kind. So our first 'Fourth' in Blue Springs was a success. I worked all summer for fifty cents per day, and took my pay in corn which the widow bought at 30 cents per bushel. I was a widower, and—well, that corn money paid our marriage fee in the spring of '60. One year I sold 500 bushels of corn at a dollar per bushel to travelers and freighters, as this is near the old road to Ft. Kearney. With that money, I bought 160 acres of land, just across the river, in '65, and sold it in '72 for $2,000. It could not now be bought for $5,000.

"The Sioux Indians gave us a scare in '61, but we all gathered together in our big house (the widow's and mine), and the twelve men of us prepared to give them battle; but they were more anxious to give battle to the Otoe Indians on the reservation.

"The Otoe Indians only bothered us by always begging for 'their poor pappoose.' My wife gave them leave to take some pumpkins out of the field, and the first thing we knew, they were hauling them away with their ponies.

"Our first religious service was in '61, by a M. E.

minister from Beatrice. Our first doctor in '63. We received our mail once a week from Nebraska City, 150 miles away. The postmaster received two dollars a year salary, but the mail was all kept in a cigar box, and everybody went and got their own mail. It afterward was carried from Mission Creek, 12 miles away, by a boy that was hired to go every Sunday morning. The U. P. R. R. was built in '80.

"My wife and I visited our friends in Eastern Pennsylvania, and surprised them with our genteel appearance. They thought, from the life we led, we would be little better than the savages. My brothers wanted me to remain east, but I felt penned up in the city where I couldn't see farther than across the street, and I told them: 'You can run out to New York, Boston, Philadelphia, and around in a few hours, but how much of this great country do you see? No, I will go back to my home on the Blue.' I am the only one of the old settlers left, and everybody calls me 'Pap Tyler.'"

I prolonged my visit until the 5th of July that I might see what the Fourth of '83 would be in Blue Springs. It was ushered in with the boom of guns and ringing of bells, and instead of the 150 of '59, there were about 4,000 gathered with the bright morning. Of course there were old ladies with bonnets, aside, and rude men smoking, but there was not that lack of intelligence and refinement one might expect to find in a country yet so comparatively new.

I thought, as I looked over the people, could our eastern towns do better? And only one intoxicated man. I marked him—fifth drunken man I have seen since entering the state. The programme of the day was as follows:

SONG—*The Red, White, and Blue.*
DECLARATION OF INDEPENDENCE—Recited by Minnie Marsham, a miss of twelve years.
SONG—*Night Before the Battle.*
TOAST—*Our Schools.* Responded to by J. C. Burch.
TOAST—*Our Railroads.* Rev. J. M. Pryse.
MUSIC—By the band.
TOAST—*Our Neighbors.* Rev. E. H. Burrington.

Rev. H. W. Warner closed the toasting with, "How, When, and Why," and with the song, "The Flag Without a Stain," all adjourned for their dinners.

Mr. and Mrs. Tyler invited me to go with them, but I preferred to eat my dinner under the flag with a stain—a rebel flag of eleven stars and three stripes—a captured relic of the late war that hung at half mast.

In afternoon they gathered again to listen to "Pap Tyler" and Pete Tom tell of the early days. But the usual 4th of July storm scattered the celebrators and spoiled the evening display of fire-works.

WYMORE

Is beautifully located near Indian Creek and Blue River. In was almost an undisturbed prairie until the B. & M. R. R. came this way in the spring of

'81, and then, Topsy-like, it "dis growed right up out of the ground," and became a railroad division town. The plot covers 640 acres, a part of which was Samuel Wymore's homestead, who settled here sixteen years ago, and it does appear that every lot will be needed.

One can scarce think that where but two years ago a dozen little shanties held all the people of Wymore, now are so many neatly built homes and even elegant residences sheltering over 2,500. To tell you what it now is would take too long. Three papers, three banks, a neat Congregational church; Methodists hold meetings in the opera hall, Presbyterians in the school-house; both expect to have churches of their own within a year; with all the business houses of a rising western town crowded in. A fine quarry of lime-stone just south on Indian Creek which has greatly helped the building up of Wymore. The heavy groves of trees along the creeks and rivers are certainly a feature of beauty. The days were oppressively warm, but the nights cool and the evenings desightful. The sunset's picture I have looked upon almost every evening here is beyond the skill of the painter's brush, or the writer's pen to portray. Truly "sunset is the soul of the day."

It is thought that in the near future Wymore and Blue Springs will shake hands across Bill creek and be one city. Success to the shake.

The Otoe Indian reservation lies but a mile south-east of Wymore. It is a tract of land that was given to the Otoe Indians in 1854, but one-half was sold five years ago. It now extends ten miles north and south, and six and three-fourths miles east and west, and extends two miles into Kansas. I will quote a few notes I took on a trip over it with Uncle John Annie, and Mary.

Left Wymore eight o'clock, drove through Blue Springs, crossed the Blue on the bridge above the mill where the river is 150 feet wide, went six miles and crossed Wild Cat creek, two miles south and crossed another creek, two miles further to Liberty, a town with a population of 800, on the B. & M. R. R., on, on, we went, going north, east, south, and west, and cutting across, and down by the school building of the agency, a fine building pleasantly located, with quite an orchard at the rear. Ate our lunch in the house that the agent had occupied.

A new town is located at the U. P. R. R. depot, yet called "the Agency." It numbers twelve houses and all built since the lands were sold the 30th of last May. Passed by some Indian graves, but I never had a "hankering" for dead Indians, so did not dig any up, as so many do. I felt real sorry that the poor Indian's last resting place was so desecrated. The men, and chiefs especially, are buried in a sitting posture, wrapped in their blankets, and their pony is killed and the head placed at the head of the grave and the tail tied to a pole and hoisted at the foot; but the women and children are buried with little ceremony, and no pony given them upon which to ride to the "happy hunting-ground."

This tribe of Indians were among the best, but warring with other tribes decreased their number until but 400 were left to take up a new home in the Indian Territory.

The land is rolling, soil black loam, and two feet or more deep; in places the grass was over a foot high. From Uncle's farm we could see Mission and Plum creeks, showing that the land is well watered. The sun was very warm, but with a covered carriage, and fanned with Nebraska breezes we were able to travel all the day. Did not reach home until the stars were shining.

For the benefit of others, I want to tell of the wisest man I ever saw working corn. I am sorry I cannot tell just how his tent was attached to his cultivator, but it was a square frame covered with muslin, and the ends hanging over the sides several inches which acted as fans; minus a hat he was taking the weather cool. Now I believe in taking these days when it says 100° in the shade, cool, and if you can't take them cool, take them as cool as you can any way. My thermometer did not do so, but left in the sun it ran as high as it could and then boiled over and broke the bulb.

There were frequent showers and one or two storms, and though they came in the night, I was up and as near ready, as I could get, for a cyclone. Aunt Jane wants me to stay until a hot wind blows for a day or two, almost taking one's breath, filling the air with dust, and shriveling the leaves. But I leave her, wiping her eyes on the corner of her apron, while she throws an old shoe after me, and with Gracie and Arthur by the hand, I go to the depot to take the 4:45 P.M. train, July 5th.

I cried once when I was bidding friends good bye, and had the rest all crying and feeling bad, so I made up my mind never to cry again at such a time if it was possible. I did not know that I would ever see these dear friends again, but I tried to think I would, and left them as though I would soon be back; and now I am going farther from home and friends.

Out from Wymore, past fields of golden grain already in the sheaf, and nicely growing corn waving in the wind. Now it is gently rolling, and now bluffy, crossing many little streams, and now a great grassy meadow. But here is what I wrote, and as it may convey a better idea of the country, I will give my notes just as I took them as I rode along:

ODELL,

A town not so large by half as Wymore. Three great long corn cribs, yet well filled. About the only fence is the snow fence, used to prevent the snow from drifting into the cuts. Grass not so tall as seen on the Reservation. Here are nicely built homes, and the beginners' cabins hiding in the cosy places. Long furrows of breaking for next year's planting. The streams are so like narrow gullies, and so covered with bushes and trees that one has to look quick and close to see the dark muddy water that covers the bottom.

DILLER,

A small town, but I know the "Fourth" was here by the bowery or dancing platforms, and the flags that still wave. Great fields of corn and grassy stretches. Am watching the banks, and I do believe the soil is running out, only about a foot until it changes to a clay. Few homes.

INDIAN CREEK.

Conductor watching to show me the noted "Wild Bill's" cabin, and now just through the cut he points to a low log cabin, where Wild Bill killed four men out of six, who had come to take his life, and as they were in the wrong and he in the right, he received much praise, for thus ridding the world of worse than useless men, and so nobly defending government property, which they wanted to take out of his hands. There is the creek running close to the cabin, and up the hill from the stream is the road that was then the "Golden Trail," no longer used by gold seekers, pony-express riders, stage drivers, wild Indians, and emigrants that then went guarded by soldiers from Fort Kearney. The stream is so thickly wooded, I fancy it offered a good hiding place, and was one of the dangerous passes in the road; but here we are at

ENDICOTT,

A town some larger than those we have passed. Is situated near the centre of the southern part of Jefferson county. Now we are passing through a very fine country with winding streams. I stand at the rear door, and watch and write, but I cannot tell all.

REYNOLDS,

A small town. Low bluffs to our left, and Rose creek to the right. Good homes and also dug-outs. Cattle-corrals, long fields of corn not so good as some I have seen. The little houses cling close to the hillsides and are hemmed about with groves of trees. Wild roses in bloom, corn and oats getting smaller again; wonder if the country is running out? Here is a field smothered with sunflowers: wonder why Oscar Wilde didn't take a homestead here? Rose creek has crossed to the left; what a wilderness of small trees and bushes follow its course! I do declare! here's a real rail fence! but not a staken-rider fence. Would have told you more about it, but was past it so soon. Rather poor looking rye and oats. Few fields enclosed with barb-wire. Plenty of cattle grazing.

HUBBELL.

Four miles east of Rose creek; stream strong enough for mill power; only one mile north of Kansas. Train stops here for supper, but I shall wait and take mine with friends in Hardy. Hubbell is in Thayer county, which was organized in 1856. Town platted in '80, on the farm of Hubbell Johnston; has a population of 450. A good school house. I have since learned that this year's yield of oats was fifty to seventy-five, wheat twenty to thirty, corn thirty to seventy-five bushels per acre in this neighborhood. I walked up main street, with pencil and book in hand, and was referred to —————— —————— for information, who asked—

"Are you writing for the *Inter Ocean?*"

"No, I am not writing for any company," I replied.

"I received a letter from the publishers a few days ago, saying that a lady would be here, writing up the Republican Valley for their publication."

I was indeed glad to know I had sisters in the same work.

We pass Chester and Harbine, and just at sunset reach Hardy, Nuckolls county. I had written to my friend, Rev. J. Angus Lowe, to meet "an old schoolmate" at the train. He had grown so tall and ministerial looking since we had last met, that I did not recognize him, and he allowed me to pass him while he peered into the faces of the men. But soon I heard some one say, "I declare, it's Belle Fulton," and grasping my hand, gives me a hearty greeting. Then he led me to his neat little home just beyond the Lutheran church, quite a nicely finished building that points its spire heavenward through his labors.

The evening and much of the night is passed before I have answered all the questions, and told all about his brothers and sisters and the friends of our native village. The next day he took his wife and three little ones and myself on a long drive into Kansas to show me the beauties of the "Garden of the West."

The Republican river leaves Nebraska a little west of Hardy, and we cross it a mile south. The water of the river is clear and sparkling, and has a rapid flow. Then over what is called "first bottom" land, with tall, waving grass, and brightened with clusters of flowers. The prettiest is the buffalo moss, a bright red flower, so like our portulacca that one would take its clusters for beds of that flower. While the sensitive rose grows in clusters of tiny, downy balls, of a faint pink, with a delicate fragrance like that of the sweet brier. They grow on a low, trailing vine, covered with fine thorns; leaves sensitive. I gathered of these flowers for pressing.

Now we are on second bottom land. Corn! Corn! It makes me tired to think of little girls dropping pumpkin seeds in but one row of these great fields, some a mile long, and so well worked, there is scarcely a weed to be seen. Some are working their corn for the last time. It is almost ready to hang its tassel in the breeze. The broad blades make one great sea of green on all sides of us. Fine timber cultures of black walnut, maple, box elder, and cottonwood. Stopped for dinner with Mrs. Stover, one of Mr. Lowe's church people. They located here some years ago, and now have a nicely improved home. I was shown their milk house, with a stream of water flowing through it, pumped by a wind-mill. Well, I thought, it is not so hard to give up our springs when one can have such conveniences as this, and have flowing water in any direction.

I was thankful to my friends for the view of the land of "smoky waters," but it seemed a necessity that I close my visit with them and go on to Red Cloud, much as I would liked to have prolonged my stay with them. Mr. Lowe said as he bade me good-bye: "You are the first one who has visited us from Pennsylvania, and it does seem we cannot have you go so soon, yet this short stay has been a great pleasure to us." I was almost yielding to their entreaties but my plans were laid, and I *must* go, and sunset saw me off.

All the country seen before dark was very pretty. Passing over a bridge I was told: "This is Dry Creek." Sure enough—sandy bed and banks, trees, bushes and bridge, everything but the water; and it is there only in wet weather.

I have been told of two streams called Lost creeks that rise five miles north-west of Hardy, and flow in parallel lines with each other for several miles, when they are both suddenly lost in a subterranean passage, and are not seen again until they flow out on the north banks of the Republican.

So, reader, if you hear tell of a Dry Creek or Lost Creek, you will know what they are.

SUPERIOR

Is a nicely built town of 800 inhabitants, situated on a plateau. The Republican river is bridged here, and a large mill built. I did not catch the name as the brakeman sang it out, and I asked of one I thought was only a mere school boy, who answered: "I did not understand, but will learn." Coming back, he informs me with much emphasis that it is Superior, and straightway goes off enlarging on the beauties and excellences of the country, and of the fossil remains he has gathered in the Republican Valley, adding: "Oh! I *just love* to go fossiling! Don't you *love* to go fossiling, Miss?"

"I don't know, I never went," I replied, and had a mind to add, "I know it is just too *lovely* for *anything.*"

It was not necessary for him to say he was from the east, we eastern people soon tell where we are from if we talk at all, and if we do not tell it in words our manners and tones do. New Englanders, New Yorkers, and Pennamites all have their own way of saying and doing things. I went to the "Valley House" for the night and took the early train next morning for McCook which is in about the same longitude as Valentine and North Platte, and thus I would go about the same distance west on all of the three railroads.

I will not tell of the way out, only of my ride on the engine. I have always greatly admired and wondered at the workings of a locomotive, and can readily understand how an engineer can learn to love his engine, they seem so much a thing of life and animation. The great throbbing heart of the Centennial—the Corliss engine, excited my admiration more than all the rest of Machinery Hall; and next to the Corliss comes the locomotive. I had gone to the round house in Wymore with my cousins and was told all about the engines, the air-brakes, and all that, but, oh, dear! I didn't know anything after all. We planned to have a ride on one before I left, but our plans failed. And when at Cambridge the conductor came in haste and asked me if I would like a ride on the engine, I followed without a thought, only that my long wished for opportunity had come. Not until I was occupying the fireman's seat did I think of what I was doing. I looked out of the window and saw the conductor quietly telling the fireman something that amused them both, and I at once knew they meant to give me "a mile a minute" ride. Well I felt provoked and ashamed that I had allowed my impulsiveness to walk me right into the cab of an engine; but I was there and it was too late to turn back, so to master the situation I appeared quite unconcerned, and only asked how far it was to Indianola.

"Fourteen miles," was the reply.

Well, the fireman watched the steam clock and shoveled in coal, and the engineer never took his eyes off the track which was as straight as a bee-line before us, and I just held on to the seat and my poke hat, and let them go, and tried to count the telegraph poles as they flew by the wrong way. After·all it was a grand ride, only I felt out of place. When nearing Indianola they ran slow to get in on time, and when they had stopped I asked what time they had made, and was answered, eighteen minutes. The conductor came immediately to help me from the cab and as he did so, asked:

"Well, did they go pretty fast?"

"I don't know, did they?" I replied.

I was glad to get back to the passenger coach and soon we were at McCook.

After the train had gone some time I missed a wrap I had left on the seat, and hastily had a telegram sent after it. After lunching at the railroad eating house, I set about gathering information about the little "Magic City" which was located May 25th 1882, and now has a population of 900. It is 255 miles east of Denver, on the north banks of the Republican river, on a gradually rising slope, while south of the river it is bluffy. It is a division station and is nicely built up with very tastily arranged cottages. Only for the newness of the place I could have fancied I was walking up Congress street in Bradford Pennsylvania. Everything has air of freshness and brightness. The first house was built in June, '82.

I am surprised at the architectural taste displayed in the new towns of the west. Surely the east is becoming old and falling behind. It is seldom a house is finished without paint; and it is a great help to the appearance of the town and country, as those who can afford a frame house, build one that will look well at a distance.

Pipes are now being laid for water works. The water is to be carried from the river to a reservoir capable of holding 40,000 gallons and located on the hill. This is being done by the Lincoln Land Company at a cost of $36,000. It has a daily and weekly paper, The McCook *Tribune,* first issued in June, '82. The printing office was then in a sod house near the river, then called Fairview postoffice, near which, about twenty farmers had gathered. The B. & M. R. R. was completed through to Colorado winter of '82. Good building stone can be obtained from Stony Point, but three miles west. McCook has its brick kiln as has almost all the towns along the way. Good clay is easily obtained, and brick is cheaper than in the east.

From a copy of the Daily *Tribune,* I read a long list of business firms and professional cards, and finished with, "*no saloons.*"

The Congregationalists have a fine church building. The Catholics worship in the Churchill House, but all other denominations are given the use of the Congregrtional church until they can build. I called upon Rev. G. Dungan, pastor of the Congregational church. He was from home, but I was kindly invited by his mother, who was just from the east, to rest in their cosy parlor. It is few of our ministers of the east that are furnished with homes such as was this minister of McCook. I was then directed to Mrs. C. C. Clark, who is superintendent of the Sunday school, and found her a lady of intelligence and refinement. She told of their Sabbath school, and of the good attendance, and how the ladies had bought the church organ, and of the society in general.

"You would be surprised to know the refinement and culture to be found in these newly built western town. If you will remain with us a few days, I will take you out into the country to see how nicely people can and do live in the sod houses and dugouts. And we will also go on an engine into Colorado. It is too bad to come so near and go back without seeing that state. Passengers very often ride on the engine on this road, and consider it a great treat; so it was only through kindness that you were invited into the cab, as you had asked the conductor to point out all that was of interest, along the way.

The rainfall this year will be sufficient for the growing of the crops, with only another good rain.

Almost everyone has bought or taken claims. One engineer has taken a homestead and timber claim, and bought 80 acres. So he has 400 acres, and his wife has gone to live on the homestead, while he continues on the road until they have money enough to go into stock-raising.

This valley does not show any sand to speak of until in the western part of Hitchcock county.

Following the winding course of the Republican river, through the eight counties of Nebraska through which it flows, it measures 260 miles. The 40th north latitude, is the south boundry line of Nebraska. As the Republican river flows through the southern tier of counties, it is easy to locate its latitude. It has a fall of 7 feet per mile, is well sustained by innumerable creeks on the north, and many from the south. These streams are more or less wooded with ash, elm, and cottonwood, and each have their cosy valley. It certainly will be a thickly populated stretch of Nebraska. The timber, the out crops of limestone, the brick clay, the rich soil, and the stock raising facilities, plenty of water and winter grazing, and the mill power of the river cannot and will not be overlooked. But hark! the train is coming, and I must go.

A Catholic priest and two eastern travelers, returning from Colorado, are the only passengers in this coach. The seats are covered with sand, and window sills drifted full. I brush a seat next to the river side and prepare to write. Must tell you first that my wrap was handed me by the porter, so if I was not in Colorado, it was.

(The prairies are dotted with white thistle flowers, that look like pond lillies on a sea of green. The buffalo grass is so short that it does not hide the tiniest flower.) Now we are alongside the river; sand-bars in all shapes and little islands of green—there it winds to the south and is lost to sight—herds of cattle—corn field—river again with willow fringed bank—cattle on a sand-bar, so it cannot be quick-sand, or they would not be there long—river gone again—tall willow grove—wire fencing—creek I suppose, but it is only a brook in width. Now a broad, beautiful valley. Dear me! this field must be five miles long, and cattle grazing in it—all fenced in until we reach

INDIANOLA,

one of the veteran towns of Red Willow county. The town-site was surveyed in 1873, and is now the county seat. Of course its growth was slow until the advent of the B. & M., and now it numbers over 400 inhabitants. "This way with your sorghum cane, and get your 'lasses' from the big sorghum mill." See a church steeple, court house, and school house—great herd of cattle—wilderness of sunflowers turning their bright faces to the sun—now nothing but grass—corral made of logs—corn and potatoes—out of the old sod into the nice new frame—river beautifully wooded—valley about four miles wide from bluff to bluff—dog town, but don't seem to be any doggies at home—board fence.

CAMBRIDGE.

Close to the bridge and near Medicine creek; population 500; a flouring mill; in Furnas county now. The flowers that I see are the prairie rose shaded from white to pink, thistles, white and pink cactuses, purple shoestring, a yellow flower, and sunflowers.

Abrupt bluffs like those of Valentine. Buffalo burs, and buffalo wallows. Country looking fine. Grain good.

ARAPAHOE.

Quite a town on the level valley; good situation. Valley broad, and bluffs a gradual rise to the tablelands; fields of grain and corn on their sloping side. This young city is situated on the most northern point of the river and twenty-two miles from Kansas, and is only forty miles from Plum creek on the Platte river, and many from that neighborhood come with their grain to the Arapahoe mills as there are two flouring mills here. It is the county-seat of Furnas county, was platted in 1871. River well timbered; corn and oats good; grain in sheaf; stumps, stumps, bless the dear old stumps! glad to see them! did'nt think any one could live in that house, but people can live in very open houses here; stakenridered fence, sod house, here is a stream no wider than our spring run, yet it cuts deep and trees grow on its banks. River close; trees—there, it and the trees are both gone south. Here are two harvesters at work, reaping and binding the golden grain.

OXFORD.

Only town on both sides of the railroad, all others are to the north; town located by the Lincoln land company; population about 400; a Baptist church; good stone for building near; damming the river for mills and factories; a creamery is being talked of. Sheep, sheep, and cattle, cattle—What has cattle? Cattle has what all things has out west. Guess what! why grass to be sure. Scenery beautiful; in Harlan county now, and we go on past Watson, Spring Hill, and Melrose, small towns, but will not be so long.

Here we are at

ORLEANS.

A beautifully situated town on a plateau, a little distance to the north; excuse, me, please, until I brush the dust from the seat before me for an old lady that has just entered the car; I am glad to have her company. Stately elms cast their shadows over a bright little stream called Elm creek that winds around at the foot of the bluff upon which the town is built. I like the scenery here very much, and, too, the town it is so nicely built. It is near the center of the county, and for a time was the county seat, and built a good court-house, but their right was disputed, and the county seat was carried to Alma, six miles east. The railroad reached this point in '80, at which time it had 400 of a population. It has advanced even through the loss of the county seat. An M. E. College, brick-yard, and grist-mill are some of its interests. Land rolling; oats ripe; buffalo grass; good grazing land. Cutting grain with oxen; a large field of barley; good bottom land; large herds and little homes; cutting hay with a reaper and the old sod's tumbled in, telling a story of trials no doubt.

ALMA.

Quite a good town, of 700 inhabitants, but it is built upon the table-land so out of sight I cannot see much of it. But this is the county seat before spoken of, and I am told is a live town.

That old lady is growing talky; has just sold her homestead near Orleans for $800, and now she is going to visit and live on the interest of her money. Came from New York ten years ago with her fatherless children. The two eastern men and myself were the only passengers in this car, so I just wrote and hummed away until I drove the men away to the end of the car where they could hear each other talking. I am so glad the old lady will talk.

REPUBLICAN CITY.

Small, but pretty town with good surrounding country. Population 400. Why, there's a wind-mill! Water must be easily obtained or they would be more plenty.

NAPONEE.

Small town. No stop here. Widespread valley; corn in tassel; grain in sheaf; wheat splendid. One flour mill and a creamery.

BLOOMINGTON—the "Highland City"—the county seat of Franklin county, and is a town like all the other towns along this beautiful valley, nicely located, and built up with beautiful homes and public buildings, and besides having large brick M. E. and Presbyterian churches, a large Normal School building, the Bloomington flour mills, a large creamery, and the U. S. land office. I am told that the Indians are excellent judges of land and are very loth to leave a good stretch of country, although they do not make much use of the rich soil. The Pawnees were the original land-holders of the Republican valley, and I do not wonder that they held so tenaciously to it. It has surely grown into a grand possession for their white brothers.

I am so tired, if you will excuse me, reader, I will just write half and use a dash for the rest of the words cor—, pota—, bush—, tre—, riv—. Wish I could make tracks on that sand bar! Old lady says "that wild sage is good to break up the ague," and I have been told it is a good preventive for malaria in any form. Driftwood! I wonder where it came from. There, the river is out of sight, and no tre— or bus—; well, I am tired saying that; going to say something else. Sensitive roses, yellow flowers, that's much better than to be talking about the river all the time. But here it is again; the most fickle stream I have ever seen! You think you will have bright waters to look upon for awhile, and just then you haven't.

But, there, we have gone five miles now, and we are at FRANKLIN, a real good solid town. First house built July, 1879. I never can guess how many people live in a town by looking at it from a car window. How do I know how many there are at work in the creamery, flouring mill, and woolen factory? And how many pupils are studying in the Franklin Academy, a fine two-story building erected by the Republican Valley Congregational Association at a cost of $3,500? First term opened Dec. 6, 1881. The present worth of the institution is $12,000, and they propose to make that sum $50,000. One hundred and seven students have been enrolled during the present term. And how many little boys and girls in the common school building? or how many are in their nicely painted homes, and those log houses, and sod houses, and dug-outs in the side of the hill, with the stovepipe sticking out of the ground? It takes all kinds of people to make a world, and all kinds of houses to make a city. Country good. Fields of corn, wheat, rye, oats, millet, broom corn, and all *sich*—good all the way along this valley.

RIVERTON.

A small town situated right in the valley. Was almost entirely laid in ashes in 1882, but Phœnix-like is rising again. Am told the B. & M. Co. have 47,000 acres of land for sale in this neighborhood at $3.50 to $10 per acre, on ten years' time and six per cent interest. Great fields of pasture and grain; wild hay lands; alongside the river now; there, it is gone to run under that bridge away over near the foot of the grassy wall of the bluffs. Why, would you believe it! here's the Republican river. Haven't seen it for a couple of minutes. But it brings trees and bushes with it, and an island. But now around the bluffs and away it goes. Reader, I have told you the "here she comes" and "there she goes" of the river to show you its winding course. One minute it would be hugging the bluffs on the north side, and then, as though ashamed of the "hug," and thought it "hadn't ought to," takes a direct south-western course for the south bluffs, and hug them awhile. Oh, the naughty river! But, there, the old lady is tired and has stopped talking, and I will follow her example. Tired? Yes, indeed! Have been writing almost constantly since I left McCook, now 119 miles away, and am right glad to hear the conductor call

RED CLOUD!

Hearing that ex-Gov. Garber was one of the early settlers of Red Cloud, I made haste to call upon him before it grew dark, for the sunbeams were already aslant when we arrived, and supper was to be eaten. As I stepped out upon the porch of the "Valley House" there sat a toad; first western toad I had seen, and it looked so like the toadies that hop over our porch at home that I couldn't help but pat it with my foot. But it hopped away from me and left me to think of home. The new moon of May had hung its golden crest over me in the valley of the Niobrara, the June moon in the valley of the Platte, and now, looking up from the Republican valley, the new July moon smiled upon me in a rather reproving way for being yet further from home than when it last came, and, too, after all my wishing. So I turned my earnest wishes into a silent prayer:

"Dear Father, take me home before the moon has again run its course!"

I found the ex-governor seated on the piazza of his cosy cottage, enjoying the beautiful evening. He received me kindly, and invited me into the parlor, where I was introduced to Mrs. Garber, a very pleasant lady, and soon I was listening to the following story:

"I was one of the first men in Webster county; came with two brothers, and several others, and took for my soldier's claim the land upon which much of Red Cloud is now built, 17th July, 1870. There were no other settlers nearer than Guide Rock, and but two there. In August several settlers came with their families, and this neighborhood was frequently visited by the Indians, who were then killing the white hunters for taking their game, and a couple had been killed near here. The people stockaded this knoll, upon which my house is built, with a wall of logs, and a trench. In this fort, 64 feet square, they lived the first winter, but I stayed in my dugout home, which you may have noticed in the side of the hill where you crossed the little bridge. I chose this spot then for my future home. I have been in many different states, but was never so well satisfied with any place as I was with this spot on the Republican river. The prairie was covered with buffalo grass, and as buffalo were very plenty, we did not want for meat. There were also plenty of elk, antelope, and deer.

"In April, '71, Webster county was organized. The commissioners met in my dug-out. At the first election there were but forty-five votes polled. First winter there were religious services held, and in the summer of '71, we had school. Our mail was carried from Hebron, Thayer county, fifty miles east. The town site was platted in October, '72, and we named it for Red Cloud, chief of the Indian tribe."

The governor looked quite in place in his elegant home, but as he told of the early days, it was hard to fancy him occupying a dug-out, and I could not help asking him how he got about in his little home, for he is a large man. He laughingly told how he had lived, his dried buffalo meat hung to the ceiling, and added:

"I spent many a happy day there."

Gov. Silas Garber was elected governor of Nebraska in 1874-6, serving well and with much honor his two terms. This is an instance of out of a dugout into the capitol. True nobility and usefulness cannot be hidden even by the most humble abode.

The home mother earth affords her children of Nebraska is much the same as the homes the great forests of the east gave to our forefathers, and have given shelter to many she is now proud to call Nebraska's children.

When I spoke of returning to the hotel, the governor said:

"We would like to have you remain with us to-night, if you will," and as Mrs. Garber added her invitation, I readily accepted their kindness, for it was not given as a mere act of form. I forgot my weariness in the pleasure of the evening, hearing the governor tell of pioneer days and doings, and Mrs. G. of California's clime and scenery—her native state.

The morning was bright and refreshing, and we spent its hours seeing the surrounding beauties of their home.

"Come, Miss Fulton, see this grove of trees I planted but eight years ago—fine, large trees they are now; and this clover and timothy; some think we cannot grow either in Nebraska, but it is a mistake," while Mrs. G. says:

"There is such a beautiful wild flower blooming along the path, and if I can find it will pluck it for you," and together we go searching in the dewy grass for flowers, while the Governor goes for his horse and phaeton to take me to the depot.

Mrs. G. is a lady of true culture and refinement, yet most unassuming and social in her manners. Before I left, they gave me a large photograph of their home. As the Governor drove me around to see more of Red Cloud before taking me to the depot, he took me by his 14x16 hillside home, remarking as he pointed it out:

"I am sorry it has been so destroyed; it might have yet made a good home for some one," then by the first frame house built in Red Cloud, which he erected for a store room, where he traded with the Indians for their furs. He hauled the lumber for this house from Grand Island, over sixty miles of trackless prairie, while some went to Beatrice, 100 miles away, for their lumber, and where they then got most of their groceries.

As we drove through the broad streets, and looked on Red Cloud from centre to suburb, I did not wonder at the touch of pride with which Governor Garber pointed out the advance the little spot of land had made that he paid for in years of service to his country.

When the B. & M. R. R. reached Red Cloud in '79, it was a town of 450 inhabitants; now it numbers 2,500. It is the end of a division of the B. & M. from Wymore, and also from Omaha; is the county seat of Webster county, and surrounded by a rich country—need I add more?

AMBOY.

A little station four miles east of Red Cloud; little stream, with bushes; and now we are crossing Dry Creek; corn looks short.

COWLES.

Beautiful rolling prairie but no timber; plenty of draws that have to be bridged; shan't write much to-day for you know it is Sunday, and I feel kind of wicked; wonder what will happen to me for traveling to-day; am listening to those travelers from the east tell to another how badly disappointed they were in Colorado. One who is an asthmatic thinks it strange if the melting at noon-day and freezing at night will cure asthma; felt better in Red Cloud than any place. Other one says he would'nt take $1,000 and climb Pike's Peak again, while others are more than repaid by the trip. A wide grassy plain to the right, with homes and groves of trees.

BLUE HILL.

A small town; great corn cribs; a level scope of country. O, rose, that blooms and wastes thy fragrance on this wide spread plain, what is thy life? To beautify only one little spot of earth, to cheer you travelers with one glance, and sweeten one breath of air; mayhap to be seen by only one out of the many that pass me by. But God sowed the seed and smiles upon me even here.

> Bloom, little flower, all the way along,
> Sing to us travelers your own quiet song.
> Speak to us softly, gently, and low,
> Are they well and happy? Flowers, do you know?

Excuse this simple rhyme, but I am so homesick.

This country is good all the way along and I do not need to repeat it so often. Nicely improved farms and homes surrounded by fine groves of trees. I see one man at work with his harvester; the only desecrator of the Sabbath I have noticed, and he may be a Seventh day Baptist.

AYR

Was but a small town, so we go on to HASTINGS, a town of over 5,000 inhabitants, and the county seat of Adams county. Is ninety-six miles west from Lincoln, and 150 miles west of the Missouri river. The B. & M. R. R. was built through Hastings in the spring of 1872, but it was not a station until the St. Joe and Denver City R. R. (now the St. Joe & Western Division of the U. P. R. R.) was extended to this point in the following autumn, and a town was platted on the homestead of W. Micklin, and named in honor of T. D. Hastings, one of the contractors of the St. Jo. & D. C. R. R. A post-office was established the same year, the postmaster receiving a salary of one dollar per month. Now, the salary is $2,100 per annum, and is the third post-office in the state for business done. It is located on a level prairie, and is nicely built up with good houses, although it has suffered badly from fires. I notice a good many windmills, so I presume water runs deep here. The surrounding country is rich farming land, all crops looking good.

Harvard, Sutton, Grafton, Fairmont, Exeter, Friend, and Dorchester, are all towns worthy of note, but it is the same old story about them all. I notice the churches are well attended.

A poor insane boy came upon the train, and showed signs of fight and, as usual, I beat a retreat to the rear of the car, but did not better my position by getting near a poor, inebriated young man, in a drunken stupor. I count him sixth, but am told he came from Denver in that condition, so I will give Colorado the honor (?) of the sixth count. I cannot but compare the two young men: The one, I am told, was a good young man, but was suddenly robbed of his reason. If it was he that was intoxicated, I would not wonder at it. I never could understand how any one in their right mind could deliberately drag themselves down to such a depth, and present such a picture of sin and shame to the world as this poor besotted one does. Everyone looks on him with contempt, as he passes up the aisle for a drink; but expressions of pity come from all for the one bereft of reason, and I ask,

Which of the two is the most insane? But I don't intend to preach a temperance sermon if it is Sunday.

CRETE,

Quite a pretty town half hid among the trees that line the Big Blue river. The valley of the Blue must be very fertile, as every plant, shrub, and tree shows a very luxuriant growth. Crete is surely a cosy retreat. The Congregational church of the state has made it a cantre of its work. Here are located Doane College and the permanent grounds of the N. S. S. A. A.

LINCOLN.

Well, here I am, and no familiar face to greet me. I asked a lady to watch my baggage for me, while I hastened to the post-office, and when I returned the train was gone and the depot closed. I stood looking through the window at my baggage inside, and turning my mind upside-down, and wrongside out, and when it was sort of crosswise and I didn't know just what to do, I asked of a man strolling around if he had anything to do with the depot. "No. I am a stranger here, and am only waiting to see the ticket agent." After explaining matters to him I asked him to "please speak to the ticket agent about that baggage for me," which he readily promised to do, and I started to walk to my friends, expecting to meet them on the way. After going some distance I thought I had placed a great deal of confidence in a stranger, and had a mind to turn back, but the sun was melting hot, and I kept right on. After I had gone over a mile, I was given a seat in a carriage of one of my friends' neighbors, and was taken to their door, and gave them another surprise, for they thought I had made a mistake in the date, as they were quite sure no train was run on that road on Sunday.

Monday. Mr. Gardner went for my baggage, but returned without it, and with a countenance too sober for joking said: "Well, your baggage is not to be found, and no one seems to know anything about it."

"Oh! Pet," "Maggie said, "I am so sorry we did not go to meet you, for this would not have happened. What did you leave?" "Everything I had." "Your silk dress too?" "Yes, but don't mention that; money would replace it, but no amount could give me back my autograph album and button string, which is filled and gathered from so many that I will never again see; and all my writings, so much that I could never replace. No, I *must* not lose it!" And then I stole away and went to Him whom I knew could help me. Some may not, but I have faith that help is given us for the minor as well as the great things of life, and as I prayed this lesson came to me—How alarmed I am over the loss of a little worldly possessions, and a few poems and scraps of writing, when so much of the heavenly possession is lost through carelessness, and each day is a page written in my life's history that will not be read and judged by this world alone, but by the Great Judge of all things. And, too, it is manuscript that cannot be altered or rewritten.

I would not allow myself to think that my baggage was gone for good, nor would I shed one tear until I was sure, and then, if gone, I would just take a good cry over it, and—but won't I hug my dusty satchels if I only get hold of them again, and never, never be so careless again. I supposed the stranger whom I had asked to speak to the ticket agent for me had improved the opportunity I gave him to secure it for his own.

So it was a rather hopeless expression that I wore, as Cousin Maggie took me to the city in the afternoon. The day was away up among the nineties, and we could not go fast. I thought, never horse traveled so slow, and felt as though I could walk, and even push to make time. But I kept quiet and didn't even say "Get up, Nellie!" I suppose a mile a minute would have been slow to me then. When at last I reached the depot my first thought was to go right to Mr. Randall with my trouble, but was told he was about to leave on the train. I peered into the faces of those gathered about the depot, but failing to find him, I turned to look at the sacred spot where I had last seen may baggage, little dreaming that I would find it, but there it all was, even my fan. "Oh dear, I am *so* glad!" and I fussed away, talking to my satchels, and telling them how glad I was to see them, and was about to give them the promised "great big hug," when I found I was attracting attention, and turning to an elderly lady I asked her to please watch my baggage for a few moments. How soon we forget our good promises to do better.—I hastened to Mr. Randall's office, found him without a thought of going away. I first told him how much I was pleased with the Republican valley, and then about my baggage.

"Why, child! did you go away and leave it here?"

"Yes, I did; and I have left it again in care of a real dressy old lady, and must go and see to it."

When I reached the waiting room the old lady and baggage were both gone. Turning to my cousin, who had just entered, I asked:

"Maggie Gardner, what did you do with that baggage?"

"Nothing; I did not know you had found it."

Then, addressing a couple who sat near, I said:

"I do wish you would tell me where that baggage went to."

"The conductor carried it away."

"Where did he go to?"

"I don't know, Miss."

Dear me; helped the old lady aboard with my baggage, I thought.

"Why, what's the matter now, Miss Fulton?" asked Mr. Randall, who had followed me. "What's gone?"

"Why, my baggage; it's gone again."

"Well, that's too bad; but come with me and perhaps we may find it in here." And we entered the baggage room just in time to save Gov. Garber's house from blowing away (the picture), but found the rest all carefully stored. Twice lost and twice found; twice sad and twice glad, and a good lesson learned.

The Burlington and Missouri River Railroad first began work at Plattsmouth, on the Missouri river, in 1869, and reached Lincoln July 20, 1870. From Lincoln it reaches out in six different lines. But this table will give a better idea of the great network of railroads under the B. & M. Co.'s control. The several divisions and their mileage are as follows:

Pacific Junction to Kearney..............196
Omaha line..................................... 17
Nebraska City to Central City...........150
Nebraska City to Beatrice................. 92
Atchison to Columbus.....................221
Crete to Red Cloud........................150
Table Rock to Wymore..................... 38
Hastings to Culbertson....................171
Denver Extension...........................244
Kenesaw cut-off to Oxford............... 77
Chester to Hebron.......................... 12
DeWitt to West Line 25
Odell to Washington, Kan............... 26
Nemaha to Salem........................... 18

The Burlington and Missouri River Railroad, being a part of the C. B. & Q. system, forms in connection with the latter road the famous "Burlington Route," known as the shortest and quickest line between Chicago and Denver, and being the only line under one management, tedious and unnecessary delays and transfers at the Missouri river are entirely avoided.

P. S. Eustis of Omaha, Neb., who is very highly spoken of, stands at the head of the B. & M. R. R. as its worthy General Passenger Agent, while R. R. Randall of Lincoln, Neb., Immigration Agent B. & M. R. R. Co., of whom I have before spoken, will kindly and most honestly direct all who come to him seeking homes in the South Platte country. His thorough knowledge of the western country and western life, having spent most of his years on the frontier, particularly qualifies him for this office.

MILFORD.

"The Saratoga of Nebraska." So termed for its beautiful "Big Blue" river, which affords good boating and bathing facilities, its wealth of thick groves of large trees, and the "dripping spring," that drips and sparkles as it falls over a rock at the river bank. As before, Mr. Randall had prepared my way, and a carriage awaited me at the depot. I was conveyed to the home of Mr. J. H. Culver, where I took tea. Mrs. Culver is a daughter of Milford's pioneer, Mr. J. L. Davison, who located at M. in 1864, and built the first house. He built a mill in '66, and from the mill, and the fording of the river at this point by the Mormons, Indians, and emigrants, was derived the name for the town that afterward grew up about him.

Through the kindness of the Davison family our stay at Milford was made very pleasant. Riding out in the evening to see the rich farming land of the valley, and in the morning a row on the river and ramble through the groves that have been a resting-place to so many weary travelers and a pleasure ground for many a picnic party. Indeed, Milford is the common resort for the Lincoln pleasure parties. It is twenty miles due west of the capital, on the B. & M. R. R., which was built in 1880. Mr. Davison told of how they had first located on Salt Creek, near where is now the city of Lincoln, but was then only wild, unbroken prairies. Finding the "Big Blue" was a better mill stream, he moved his stakes and drove them deep for a permanent home on its banks. He first built a log house, and soon a frame, hauling his lumber from Plattsmouth. A saw-mill was soon built on the "Blue," and lumber was plenty right at hand. The ford was abandoned for a bridge he built in '66, and to his flouring-mill came grain for a hundred miles away, as there was none other nearer than Ashland. This being the principal crossing-place of the Blue, all the vegetables they could raise were readily sold. Mrs. Culver told of selling thirty-five dollars' worth of vegetables from her little garden patch in one week, adding: "We children were competing to see who could make the most from our garden that week, and I came out only a few dollars ahead of the rest."

Mrs. D. told of how with the aid of a large dog, and armed with a broom, she had defended a neighbor's daughter from being carried away captive by a band of Indians. The story of their pioneering days was very interesting, but space will not allow me to repeat it.

In the morning I was taken through three very pretty groves. One lies high on a bluff, and is indeed a pretty spot, named "Shady Cliff." Then winding down canyon Seata, *little* canyon, we crossed the River to the Harbor, an island which is covered with large cottonwood, elm, hickory, and ash, and woven among the branches are many grapevines—one we measured being sixteen inches in circumference—while a cottonwood measured eighteen feet in circumference. Surely it has been a harbor where many weary ones have cast anchor for a rest. (Another grove, the Retreat, is even more thickly wooded and vined over, and we found its shade a very pleasant retreat on that bright sunny morning.) But pleasanter still was the row of a mile down the river to the "Sparkling Springs."

Reader, go ask Professor Aughey about the rocks over which this spring flows. All I can tell you is, it looks like a great mass of dark clay into which had been stirred an equal quantity of shells of all sizes, but which had decayed and left only their impression on the hardened rock.

The river is 100 feet wide and has a rock bottom which makes it fine for bathing in, and the depth and volume of water is sufficient for the running of small steamers. School was first held in Mr. Davison's house in '69. The first church was erected by the Congregational society in '69. First newspaper was established in '70, by J. H. Culver, and gained a state reputation under the name of the "Blue Valley *Record.*" Rev. H. A. French began the publication of the " *Congregational News*" in '78.

The "Milford *Ozone*" is the leading organ of the day, so named for the health-giving atmosphere that the Milfordites enjoy.

A post-office was established in '66, J. S. Davison acting as postmaster. Mail was received once a week from Nebraska City, via Camden. The mail was distributed from a dry goods box until in '70, J. H. Culver was appointed postmaster, and a modern post-office was established.

The old mill was destroyed by fire in '82, and is now replaced by a large stone and brick building costing $100,000, and has a capacity of 300 barrels per day. The population of Milford is about 600. We cross the iron bridge that now spans the river to the east banks and take a view of the new town of EAST MILFORD laid out on an eighty acre plot that borders on the river and gradually rises to the east. It is a private enterprise to establish a larger town on this particularly favored spot, where those who wish may have a home within easy reach of the capital and yet have all the beauty and advantage of a riverside home. I could scarcely resist the temptation to select a residence lot and make my home on the beautiful Blue, the prettiest spot I have yet found in Nebraska.

CHAPTER V.

NEBRASKA AND HER CAPITAL.

Nebraska is so named from the Nebraska, or Platte river. It is derived from the Indian *ne* (water) and *bras* (shallow), and means shallow water. In extent it is 425 miles from east to west, and 138 to 208 from north to south, and has an area of 75.995 square miles that lie between parallels 40° and 43° north latitude, and 18° and 27° west longitude.

The Omahas, Pawnees, Otoes, Sioux, and other Indian tribes were the original land-holders, and buffalo, elk, deer, and antelope the only herds that grazed from its great green pasture lands. But in 1854, "Uncle Sam" thought the grassy desert worthy of some notice, and made it a territory, and in 1867 adopted it as the 37th state, and chose for its motto "*Equality before the Law.*"

The governors of Nebraska territory were:
Francis Burt, 1854.
T. B. Cuming, 1854–5.
Mark W. Izard, 1855–8.
W. A. Richardson, 1858.
J. S. Morton, 1858–9.
Samuel W. Black, 1859–61.
Alvin Saunders, 1861–6.
David Butler, 1866–7.

Of the state—
   David Butler, 1867–71.
   William H. James, 1871–3.
   Robert W. Furnas, 1873–5.
   Silas Garber, 1875–9.
   Albinus Nance, 1879–83.
   James W. Dawes, 1883.

Allow me to quote from the *Centennial Gazetteer of United States:*

"SURFACE.—Nebraska is a part of that vast plain which extends along the eastern base of the Rocky mountains, and gently slopes down toward the Missouri river. The surface is flat or gently undulating. There are no ranges or elevations in the state that might be termed mountains. The soil consists for the most part of a black and porous loam, which is slightly mixed with sand and lime. The streams flow in deeply eroded valleys with broad alluvial flood grounds of the greatest fertility, which are generally well timbered with cottonwood, poplar, ash, and other deciduous trees. The uplands are undulating prairie. Late surveys establish the fact that the aggregate area of the bottom lands is from 13,000,000 to 14,000,000 of acres.

"THE CLIMATE of Nebraska is on the whole similar to that of other states of the great Mississippi plains in the same latitude. The mean annual temperature varies from 47° in the northern sections to 57° in the most southern. But owing to greater elevation, the western part of the state is somewhat colder than the eastern. In winter the westerly winds sweeping down from the Rocky mountains, often depress the thermometer to 20° and sometimes 30° below zero; while in the summer a temperature of 100° and over is not unusual. In the southern tier of counties the mean temperature of the summer is 76¼°, and of winter, 30½°. The greatest amount of rain and snow fall (28 to 30 inches) falls in the Missouri valley, and thence westward the rainfall steadily decreases to 24 inches near Fort Kearney, 16 inches to the western counties, and 12 inches in the south-western corner of the state.

"POPULATION.—Nebraska had in 1860 a population of 28,841, and in 1870, 122,993. Of these, 92-245 were natives of the United States, including 18,-425 natives of the state. The foreign born population numbered 30,748.

"EDUCATION.— Nebraska has more organized schools, more school houses, and those of a superior character; more money invested in buildings, books, etc., than were ever had before in any state of the same age. The land endowed for the public schools embraces one-eighteenth of the entire area of the state—2,623,080 acres." The school lands are sold at not less than seven dollars per acre, which will yield a fund of not less than $15,000,000, and are leased at from six to ten per cent interest on a valuation of $1.25 to $10 per acre. The principal is invested in bonds, and held inviolate and undiminished while the interest and income alone is used.

The state is in a most excellent financial condition, and is abundantly supplied with schools, churches, colleges, and the various charitable and reformatory institutions. Every church is well represented in Nebraska. The Methodist stands first in numbers, while the Presbyterian, Baptist, and Congregational are of about equal strength. The Catholic church is fully represented.

The United States census for 1880 shows that Nebraska has the lowest percentage of illiteracy of any state in the Union. Iowa comes second. Allow me to compare Nebraska and Pennsylvania:

Nebraska, 1.73 per cent cannot read, 2.55 per cent cannot write; Pennsylvania, 3.41 per cent cannot read, 5.32 per cent cannot write. Total population of Nebraska, 452,402; Pennsylvania, 4,282,891.

Geographically, Nebraska is situated near the centre of the United States, and has an average altitude of 1,500 feet above the level of the sea, varying from 1,200 feet at the Missouri river to 2,000 feet at the Colorado state line. The climate of Nebraska is noted for its salubrity, its wholesomeness, and healthfulness. The dryness of the air, particularly in the winter, is the redeeming feature of the low temperature that is sometimes very suddenly brought about by strong, cold winds, yet the average temperature of the winter of 1882 was but 17°, and of the summer 70°.

I only wish to add that I have noticed that the western people in general have a much healthier and robust appearance than do eastern people.

Later statistics than the United States census of 1880 are not accessible for my present purpose, but the figures of that year—since which time there has been rapid developments—will speak volumes for the giant young state, the youngest but one in the Union.

The taxable values of Nebraska in 1880 amounted to $90,431,757, an increase of nearly forty per cent in ten years, being but $53,709,828 in 1870. During the same time its population had increased from 122,933 to 452,542, nearly four-fold.

The present population of Nebraska probably exceeds 600,000, and its capacity for supporting population is beyond all limits as yet. With a population as dense as Ohio, or seventy-five persons to the square mile, Nebraska would contain 5,700,000 souls. With as dense a population as Massachusetts, or 230 to the square mile, Nebraska would have 17,480,000 people.

The grain product of Nebraska had increased from 10,000 bushels in 1874 to 100,000 bushels in 1879, an average increase of 200 per cent per year. In 1883 there was raised in the state:

Wheat...................................... 27,481,300.
Corn .... 101,276,000.
Oats... 21,630,000.

Mr. D. H. Wheeler, secretary of the state board

of agriculture, has prepared the following summary of all crop reports received by him up to Nov. 13, 1883:

Corn, yield per acre	41 bushels.
Quality	85 per cent.
Potatoes, Irish	147 bushels.
Quality	109 per cent.
Potatoes, sweet	114 bushels.
Quality	111 per cent.
Hay, average tame and wild	2 tons per a.
Quality	107 per cent.
Sorghum, yield per acre	119 gallons.
Grapes, yield and quality	88 per cent.
Apples, yield and quality	97 per cent.
Pears, yield and quality	52 per cent.
Condition of orchards	100 per cent.
Spring wheat threshed at date	82 per cent.

Grade of Spring wheat, No. 2. First frost, Oct. 5. Corn ready for market, Dec. 1.

In 1878 there were raised in the state 295,000 hogs, and in 1879 a total of 700,000, an increase of nearly 250 per cent. There are raised annually at the present time in Nebraska over 300,000 cattle and 250,000 sheep.

The high license liquor law was pasesd in Nebraska in 1883, requiring the paying of $1,000 for license to sell liquor in a town of 1,000 inhabitants or more, and $500 elsewhere, all of which is thrown into the common school fund and must be paid before a drink is sold. Liquor dealers and saloon keepers are responsible for all damages or harm done by or to those to whom they have sold liquor while under its influence.

During my stay of almost three months in the state, I saw but seven intoxicated men and I looked sharp and counted every one who showed the least signs of having been drinking. There are but few hotels in the state that keep a bar. I did not learn of one. Lincoln has 18,000 of a population and but twelve saloons. Drinking is not popular in Nebraska.

I will add section 1 of Nebraska's laws on the rights of married women.

"The property, real and personal, which any woman in this state may own at the time of her marriage, and the rents, issues, profits, or proceeds thereof, and any real, personal, or mixed property which shall come to her by descent, devise, or the gift of any person except her husband, or which she shall acquire by purchase or otherwise, shall remain her sole and separate property, notwithstanding her marriage, and shall not be subject to the disposal of her husband, or liable for his debts."

"The property of the husband shall not be liable for any debt contracted by the wife before marriage."

The overland pony express, which was the first regular mail transportation across the state, was started in 1860 and lasted two years. The distance from St.

Joseph, Missouri, to San Francisco was about 2,000 miles and was run in thirteen days. The principal stations were St. Joseph and Marysville, Mo.; Ft. Kearney, Neb.; Laramie and Ft. Bridger, Wy. T.; Salt Lake, Utah; Camp Floyd and Carson City, Nev.; Placerville, Sacramento, and San Francisco, Cal. Express messengers left once a week with ten pounds of matter; salary $1,200 per month; carriage on one-fourth ounce was five dollars in gold. But in the two years the company's loss was $200,000. Election news was carried from St. Joseph, Mo., to Denver City, Col., a distance of 628 miles in sixty-nine hours. A telegraph line was erected in Nebraska, 1862; now Nebraska can boast of nearly 3,000 miles of railroad.

I want to say that I find it is the truly energetic and enerprising people who come west. People who have the energy and enterprise that enable them to leave the old home and endure the privations of a new country for a few years that they may live much better in the "after while," than they could hope to do in the old home, and are a people of ambition and true worth. The first lesson taught to those who come west by those who have gone before and know what it is to be strangers in a strange land, is true kindness and hospitality, and but few fail to learn it well and profit by it, and are ready to teach it by precept and example to those who follow. It is the same lesson our dear great-grandfathers and mothers learned when they helped to fell the forests and make a grand good state out of "Penn's Woods." But their children's children are forgetting it. Yet I find that Pennsylvania has furnished Nebraska with some of her best people. Would it not be a good idea for the Pennamites of Nebraska to each year hold Pennsylvania day, and every one who come from the dear old hills, meet and have a general hand-shaking and talk with old neighbors and friends. I know Nebraska could not but be proud of her Pennsylvanian children.

LINCOLN.

In 1867 an act was passed by the state legislature, then in session at Omaha, appointing a commission consisting of Gov. Butler, Secretary of State T. P. Kennard, and Auditor of State J. Gillespie to select and locate a new capital out on the frontier. After some search the present *capital* site was chosen—then a wild waste of grasses, where a few scattered settlers gathered at a log cabin to receive the mail that once a week was carried to them on horseback to the Lancaster post-office of Lancaster county. The site is 65 miles west of the Missouri river, and 1,114 feet above sea level, and on the "divide" between Antelope and Salt Creeks. 900 acres were platted into lots and broad streets, reserving ample ground for all necessary public buildings, and the new capital was named in honor of him for whom Columbia yet mourned. Previous to the founding of Lincoln by the state, a Methodist minister named Young had selected a part of the land, and founded a paper town and called it Lancaster.

The plan adopted for the locating of the capital of the new state was as follows: The capital should be located upon lands belonging to the state, and the money derived from the sale of the lots should build all the state buildings and institutions. After the selection by the commission there was a slight rush for town lots, but not until the summer of '68 was the new town placed under the auctioneer's hammer, which, however, was thrown down in disgust as the bidders were so few and timid. In 1869, Col. George B. Skinner conducted a three days' sale of lots, and in that time sold lots to the amount of $171,000. When he received his wages—$300—he remarked that he would not give his pay for the whole town site.

The building boom commenced at once, and early in '69 from 80 to 100 houses were built. The main part of the state house was begun in '67, but the first legislature did not meet at the new capitol until in January, '69. From the sale of odd numbered blocks a sufficient sum was realized to build the capitol building, costing $64,000, the State University, $152,000, and State Insane Asylum $137,500, and pay all other expenses and had left 300 lots unsold.

The State Penitentiary was built at a cost of $312,-000 in 1876. The post-office, a very imposing building, was erected by the national government at a cost of $200,000, finished in '78. Twenty acres were reserved for the B. & M. depot. It is ground well occupied. The depot is a large brick building 183x53 and three stories high, with lunch room, ladies' and gents' waiting rooms nicely furnished, baggage room, and broad hall and stairway leading to the telegraph and land offices on the second and third floors. Ten trains arrive and depart daily carrying an aggregate of 1,400 passengers. The U. P. has ample railway accommodations.

All churches and benevolent societies that applied for reservation were given three lots each, subject to the approval of the legislature, which afterward confirmed the grant. A Congregational church was organized in 1866; German Methodist, '67; Methodist Episcopal and Roman Catholic, '68; Presbyterian, Episcopal, Baptist, and Christian, '69; Universalist, '70; African Methodist, '73, and Colored Baptist, '79. A number have since been added.

THE STATE JOURNAL CO. On the 15th of Aug., 1867, the day following the announcement that Lancaster was *the place* for the capital site there appeared in the *Nebraska City Press* a prospectus for the publication of a weekly newspaper in Lincoln, to be called the *Nebraska Commonwealth*, C. H. Gere, Editor. But not until the latter part of Nov. did it have an established office in the new city. In the spring of '69 the *Commonwealth* was changed to the Nebraska

State Journal. As a daily it was first issued on the 20th of July, '70, the day the B. & M. R. R. ran its first train into Lincoln, and upset all the old stage coaches that had been the only means of transportation to the capital. In '82 the State Journal Co. moved into their handsome and spacious new building on the corner of P and 9th streets. It is built of stone and brick, four stories high, 75 feet on P and 143 on 9th streets. The officers are C. H. Gere, Pres.; A. H. Mendenhall, Vice Pres.; J. R. Clark, Sec., and H. D. Hathaway, Treas. The company employs 100 to 125 hands. Beside the *Journal* are the *Democrat* and *News*, daily; the *Nebraska Farmer*, semi monthly; the *Capital*, weekly; the *Hesperian Student*, monthly, published by the students of the University, and the *Staats Anzeiger*, a German paper, issued weekly.

On my return from Milford, Wednesday, I sought and found No. 1203 G street, just in time to again take tea with the Keefer family, and spend the night with them, intending to go to Fremont next day. But Mrs. K. insisted that she would not allow me to slight the capital in that way, and to her I am indebted for much of my sight-seeing in and about Lincoln.

Thursday afternoon we went to the penitentiary to see a little of convict life. But the very little I saw made me wonder why any one who had once suffered imprisonment would be guilty of a second lawless act. Two negro convicts in striped uniforms were lounging on the steps ready to take charge of the carriages, for it was visitor's day. Only good behaved prisoners, whose terms have almost expired, are allowed to step beyond the iron bars and stone walls. We were taken around through all the departments —the kitchen, tailor shop, and laundry, and where brooms, trunks, harnesses, corn-shellers, and much that I cannot mention, are made. Then there was the foundry, blacksmith shop, and stone yard, where stones were being sawed and dressed ready for use at the capitol building. The long double row of 160 cells are so built of stone and cement that when once the door of iron bars closes upon a prisoner he has no chance of exit. They are 4x7 feet, and furnished with an iron bedstead, and one berth above; a stool, and a lap-board to write on. They are allowed to write letters every three weeks, but what they write is read before it is sent, and what they receive is read before it is given to them. There are 249 prisoners, a number of whom are from Wyoming. Their meals are given them as they pass to their cells. They were at one time seated at a table and given their meals together, but a disturbance arose among them and they used the knives and forks for weapons to fight with. And they carried them off secretly to their cells, and one almost succeeded in cutting his way through the wall. Only those who occupy the same cell can hold any conversation. Never a word is allowed to be exchanged outside the cells with each other. Thus silently, like a noiseless machine, with bowed heads, not even exchanging a word, and scarcely a glance, with their elbow neighbor, they work the long days through, from six o'clock until seven, year in and year out. On the Fourth of July they are given two or three hours in which they can dance, sing, and talk to each other, a privilege they improve to the greatest extent, and a general handshaking and meeting with old neighbors is the result. Sunday, at nine A. M., they are marched in close file to the chapel, where Rev. Howe, City Missionary, formerly a missionary in Brooklyn and New York, gives them an hour of good talk, telling them of Christ and Him Crucified, and of future reward and punishment, but no sectarian doctrines. He assures me some find the pearl of great price even within prison walls. They have an organ in the chapel and a choir composed of their best singers, and it is not often we hear better. Rev. Howe's daughter often accompanies her father and sings for them. They are readily brought to tears by the singing of Home, Sweet Home, and the dear old hymns. Through Mr. Howe's kind invitation we enjoyed his services with them, and as we rapped for admittance behind the bars, the attendant said: "Make haste, the boys are coming"; and the iron door was quickly locked after we entered. A prisoner brought us chairs, and we watched the long line of convicts marching in, the right hand on the shoulder of the one before them, and their striped cap in the left. They filed into the seats and every arm was folded. It made me sigh to see the boyish faces, but a shudder would creep over me when, here and there, I marked a number wearing the hoary locks of age. As I looked into their faces I could not but think of the many little children I have talked to in happy school days gone by, and my words came back to me: "Now, children, remember I will never forget you, and I will always be watching to see what good men and women you make; great philanthropists, teachers, and workers in the good work, good ministers, noble doctors, lawyers that will mete out true justice, honest laborers, and who knows but that a future Mr. or Mrs. President sits before me on a school bench? Never, never allow me to see your name in disgrace." And I hear a chorus of little voices answer: "I'll be good, Teacher, I'll be good." But before me were men who, in their innocent days of childhood, had as freely and well-meaningly promised to be good. But the one grand thought brightened the dark picture before me: God's great loving-kindness and tender mercy—a God not only to condemn but to forgive. Nine-tenths of the prisoners, I am told, are here through intemperance. Oh, ye liquor dealers that deal out ruin with your rum by the cask or sparkling goblet! Ye poor wretched drunkard, social drinker, or fashionable tippler! Why

ERRATA.

Page 245, last line but one, in place of "Nebraska is visited" read "Nebraska is *not* visited." Third line from bottom leave out the word "not" from commencement of line.

cannot you be men, such as your Creator intended you should be? I sometimes think God will punish the *cause,* while man calls the effect to account. For my part, I will reach out my hand to help raise the poorest drunkard from the ditch rather than to shake hands with the largest liquor dealer in the land, be he ever so good (?) Good! He knows what he deals out, and that mingled with his ill-gotten gains is the taint of ruined souls, souls for which he will have to answer for before the Great Judge who never granted a license to sin, nor decided our guilt by a jury.

Mrs. K. had secured a pass to take us to the insane asylum, but we felt we had seen enough of sadness, and returned home.

Friday. About two P.M. the sky was suddenly darkened with angry looking clouds, and I watched them with interest as they grew more threatening and the thunder spoke in louder tones. I was not anxious to witness a cyclone, but if one *must* come, I wanted to watch its coming, and see all I could of it. But the winds swept the clouds rapidly by, and in a couple of hours the streets were dry, and we drove out to see the only damage done, which was the partial wreck of a brick building that was being erected. Reports came in of a heavy fall of hail a few miles west that had the destroyed corn crop not in some places. This was the hardest storm seen during my stay in the state. Nebraska is visited, as some suppose, with the terrible cyclones and wind storms that sweep over some parts of the West; nor have I experienced the constant wind that I was told of before I came; yet Nebraska has more windy weather than does Pennsylvania.

The sun comes down with power, and when the day is calm, is very oppressive; but the cool evenings revive and invigorate all nature.

Saturday we spent in seeing the city from center to suburb and drinking from the artesian well in the government square. The water has many medical properties, and is used as a general "cure-all."

Climbing the many steps to the belfry of the University, we had a fine view of the city, looking north, east, south, and west, far over housetops. Many are fine buildings of stone and brick, and many beautiful residences with well kept lawns. The streets are 100 and 120 feet wide. Sixteen feet on each side are appropriated for sidewalks, five of which, in all but the business streets, is the walk proper—built of stone, brick, or plank—and the remaining eleven feet are planted with shade trees, and are as nicely kept as the door yards.

The streets running north and south are numbered from first to twenty-fifth street. Those from east to west are lettered from A to W.

Saturday evening—a beautiful moonlight night—just such a night as makes one wish for a ride. Who can blame me if I take one? A friend has been telling how travelers among the Rockies have to climb the mountains on mountain mules or burros. My curiosity is aroused to know if when I reach the foot of Pike's Peak, I can ascend. It would be aggravating to go so far and not be able to reach the Peak just because I couldn't ride on a donkey. So Mrs. K. engaged Gussie Chapman, a neighbor's boy, to bring his burro over *after dark*. All saddled, Fanny waits at the door, and I must go.

Good bye, reader, I'll tell you all about my trip when I get back—I'll telegraph you at the nearest station. Don't be uneasy about me; I am told that burros never run off, and if Fanny should throw me I have only three feet to fall. I wonder what her great ears are for—but a happy thought strikes me, and I hang my poke hat on one and start.

> One by one her feet are lifted,
> One by one she sets them down;
> Step by step we leave the gatepost,
> And go creeping 'round to a convenient puddle,

when Fanny flops her ears, and lands my hat in the middle. Well, you cannot expect me to write poetry and go at this rate of speed. My thoughts and the muses can't keep pace with the donkey.

Most time to telegraph back to my friends who waved me away so grandly. But, dear me, I have been so lost in my reverie on the lovely night, and thoughts of how I could now climb Pike's Peak—*if I ever reached the foot of the mountain,*—that I did not notice that Fanny had crept round the mud puddle, and was back leaning against the gate-post. Another start, and Fanny's little master follows to whip her up; but she acts as though she wanted to slide me off over her ears, and I beg him to desist, and we will just creep. Poor little brute, you were created to creep along the dangerous mountain passes with your slow, cautious tread, and I won't try to force you into a trot.

Well, I went up street and down street, and then gave my seat to Hettie Keefer.

"What does it eat?" I asked.

"Oh, old shoes and rags, old tin cans, and just anything at all."

I wish I could tell you all about this queer little Mexican burro, but Hettie is back, and it is time to say good night.

In 1880, Kansas was so flooded with exodus negroes that Nebraska was asked to provide for a few, and over one hundred were sent to Lincoln. Near Mr. K.'s home, they have a little church painted a crushed strawberry color, and in the afternoon, our curiosity led us right in among these poor negroes so lately from the rice and cotton fields and cane brakes of the sunny South, to see and hear them in their worship. They call themselves Baptist, but, ignorant of their church belief, requested the Rev. Mr. Gee, then minister of the Lincoln Baptist church, to come and baptise their infants.

I went supplied with a large fan to hide a smiling

countenance behind, but had no use for it in that way. Their utter ignorance, and yet so earnest in the very little they knew, drove all the smiles away, and I wore an expression of pity instead.

The paint is all on the outside of the house, and the altar, stand and seats are of rough make up. The whole audience turned the whites of their eyes upon us as we took a seat near the door. Soon a powerful son of Africa arose and said:

/"Bruddering, I havn't long to maintain ye, but if ye'll pray for me for about the short space of fifteen minutes, I'll try to talk to ye. And Moses lifted up his rod in de wilderness, dat all dat looked upon dat rod might be healed. Now in dose days dey had what they called sarpents, but in dese days we call dem snakes, and if any one was bit by a snake and would look on dat rod he would be healed of de snake bite." How earnestly he talk to his "chilens" for de short space of time, until he suddenly broke off and said with a broad grin: "Now my time is up. Brudder, will you pray?" And while the brudder knelt in prayer the audience remained seated, hid their faces in their hands, and with their elbows resting on their knees, swayed their bodies to a continual humumum, and kept time with their feet; the louder the prayer, the louder grew the hum until the prayer could not be heard. One little Topsy sat just opposite us keeping time to the prayer by bobbing her bare heels up and down from a pair of old slippers much too large for her, showing the ragged edges of a heelless stocking, while she eyed "de white folks in de corner." After prayer came the singing, if such it may be called. The minister lined out a hymn from the only hymn book in the house, and as he ended the last word he began to sing in the same breath, and the rest followed. It did not matter whether it was long, short, or particular meter, they could drawl out one word long enough to make six if necessary, and skip any that was in the way. It was only a perfect mumble of loud voices that is beyond description, and must be heard to be appreciated. But the minister cut the singing short, by saying: "Excuse de balance," which we were glad to do. I was very much afraid he was getting "Love among the roses" mixed in with the hymn. While they sang, a number walked up to the little pine table and threw down their offering of pennies and nickels with as much pride and pomp as though they gave great sums, some making two trips. Two men stood at the table and reached out each time a piece of money was put down to draw it into the pile; but with all their caution they could not hinder one girl from taking up, no doubt, more than she put down, and not satisfied with that, again walked up and quickly snatched a piece of money without even pretending to throw some down. The minister closed with a benediction, and then announced that "Brudder Alexander would exhort to ye to-night and preach de gospel pint forward; and if de Lord am willin, I'll be here too."

A number gathered around and gave us the right hand of fellowship with an invitation to come again, which we gladly accepted, and evening found us again in the back seat with pencil and paper to take notes.

Brudder Alexander began with: "Peace be unto dis house while I try to speak a little space of time, while I talks of brudder Joshua. My text am de first chapter of Joshua, and de tenth verse. 'Then Joshua commanded the officers of the people, saying,' Now Joshua was a great wrastler and a war-man, and he made de walls of Jericho to fall by blowen on de horns. Oh, chilens! and fellow-mates, neber forget de book of Joshua. Look-yah! Simon Peta was de first bishop of Rome, but de Lord had on old worn-out clothes, and was sot upon an oxen, and eat moldy bread. And look-a-yah! don't I member de time, and don't I magine it will be terrible when de angel will come wid a big horn, and he'll give a big blah on de horn, and den look out; de fire will come, and de smoke will descend into heaven, and de earth will open up its mouth and not count the cost of houses. And look-a-yah! I hear dem say, de Rocky mountains will fall on ye. Oh, bruddering and fellow-mates, I clar I heard dem say, if ye be a child of God, hold out and prove faithful, and ye'll receive the crown, muzzle down. Now chilen, my time is expended."

And with this we left them to enjoy their prayer meeting alone, while we came home, ready to look on the most ridiculous picture that can be drawn by our famous artist in Blackville, and believe it to be a true representation. Poor children, no wonder the "true blue" fought four long years to set you free from a life of bondage that kept you in such utter ignorance.

Monday morning I felt all the time I had for Lincoln had been "expended," and I bade my kind friends of the capital good-bye.

CHAPTER VI.

Home again from Lincoln, Nebraska, to Indiana County Pennsylvania. The Kinzua bridge and Niagara Falls.—The conclusion.

Left Lincoln Monday morning, July 17, on the U. P. R. R. for Fremont. Passed fields of corn almost destroyed by the hail storm of last Friday. It is sad to see some of the farmers cultivating the stubble of what but a few days ago was promising fields of corn. We followed the storm belt until near Wahoo, where we again looked on fine fields. At Valley, a small town, we changed cars and had a tiresome wait of a couple of hours. I was surprised to see a town in Nebraska that seemed to be on the stand-still, but was told that it was too near Omaha and Fremont. A short ride from Valley brought us to Fremont. The first person I saw at the depot was Mrs. Euber, one of the colonists. Before she had reccognized me, I put my arm about her and said: "Did you come to meet me, Mrs. Euber?"

"Why, Sims, is this you! I thought you had gone back east long ago."

After promising to spend my time with her, I went to speak to Mr. Reynolds, to whom I had written that I expected to be in Fremont the previous week.

"Well," he said, "you have a great sin to answer for; when I received your card, I ordered a big bill of groceries, and Mrs. Reynolds had a great lot of good things prepared for your entertainment; and when you didn't come, I almost killed myself eating them up."

Sorry I had missed such a treat; and caused so much misery. I left him, promising to call for any he might have left, which I did, and I found he had not eaten them all—which quite relieved my guiltiness. I called on Mrs. N. Turner, one of Fremont's earliest settlers, from whom I learned much of the early history of the country. She said as she shook my hand at parting: "I sincerly hope you will have a safe journey home, and find your dear mother well!"

"Thank you," I replied, "you could not have wished me any thing better." Nothing can be more pleasant to me than to thus snatch acquaintances here and there, and though 'tis but a very short time we meet, yet I reap many good impressions, and many pleasing memories are stored away for future reference, in quiet hours.

Left Fremont Wednesday noon, July 19, with aching temples; but the thought that I was really going home at last, soon relieved my indisposition, and I was ready to write as I went; eastward bound, over level country of good pasture and hay lands. Land, that, when we passed over the 26th April was void of a green spear; trees that then swayed their budding branches in the winds, now toss their leafy boughs. Said good-bye to the winding Elkhorn river, a little way east of Fremont.

Wild roses and morning glories brighten the way. Why! here we are at Blair; but I have told of Blair before, so will go on to the Missouri river. And as we cross over I stand on the platform of the rear car where I can see the spray, and as I look down into the dark water and watch the furrow the boat leaves in the waves, I wonder where are all those that crossed over with me to the land I have just left. Some have returned, but the majority have scattered over the plains of Northwestern Nebraska. I was aroused from my sad reverie by an aged gentleman who stood in the door, asking: "Why, is this the way we cross the river? My! how strong the water must be to bear us up! Oh, dear! Be careful, Sis, or you might fall off when the boat jars against the shore."

"I am holding tight," I replied, "and if I do I will fall right in the boat or skiff swung at the stern." I did not then know that to fall into the Missouri river is almost sure death, as the sand that is mixed with the water soon fills the clothing, and carries one to bottom— but we landed without a jar or jolt and leave the muddy waves for the sandy shores of Iowa.

Reader, I wish I could tell you all about my home going—of my visit at Marshalltown, Iowa, with the Pontious family—dear old friends of my grandparents; at Oswego, Ill., with an uncle; at Tiffin and Mansfield, Ohio, with more friends, and all I heard and saw along the way. Allow me to skip along and only sketch the way here and there.

July 30, 5:30 P.M. "Will you tell me, please, when we cross the Pennsylvania state line?" I asked of the conductor. "Why, we crossed the line ten miles back." And I just put my hand out of the window and shake hands with the dear old state and throw a kiss to the hills and valleys, and that rocky bank covered with flowering vines. I thought there was an air of home in the breezes.

The sun was going down, and shadows growing long when we stopped at Meadville, and while others took supper I walked to the rear of the depot to the spot where our party had snow-balled only three months ago. The snow has melted, the merry party widely separated, and alone I gather leaves that then were only buds, and think. Ah! their bright expectations were all in the bud then. Have they unfolded into leaves as bright as these I gather?

Well, I am glad to pat the soil of my native state, and call it dear old "Pa." But could my parents go with me I feel I would like to return again to Nebraska, for though I could never love it as I always shall the "Keystone," yet I have already learned to very highly respect and esteem Nebraska for its worth as a state, and for the kind, intelligent people it holds within its arms.

As I take my seat in the car, a young, well-dressed boy sits near me in a quiet state of intoxication. Well, I am really ashamed! To think I have seen two drunken men to-day and only seven during my three months' stay in Nebraska. So much good for the high license law. If you cannot have prohibition, have the next best thing, and drowned out all the little groggeries and make those who *will* have it, pay the highest price. Poor boy! You had better go to Nebraska and take a homestead.

"Old Sol" has just hid his face behind the dear old hills and it is too dark to see, so I sing to myself. My "fellow mates" hear the hum and wonder what makes me so happy. They don't know I am going home, do they?

"Salamanaca! change cars for Bradford," and soon I am speeding on to B. over the R. & P. road. Two young men and myself are the sole occupants of the car.

"Where do you stop when you go to B.?" one asks of the other.

"At the —— (naming one of the best hotels) generally, but they starve a fellow there. In fact, they do at all the hotels; none of them any good."

"Well, that's just my plain opinion," No. 1 answers, and I cuddle down to sleep, fully assured that I am really near Bradford, where everything is "no good," and "just too horrid for anything." Suppose those young dandies are "Oil Princes"—"Coal

Oil Johnnies," you know—and can smash a hotel just for the amusement, but can't pay for their fun.

When I arrived at Bradford the young men watched me tug at my satchels as I got off, all alone, in the darkness of the midnight hour. I knew my brother would not be expecting me, and had made up my mind to take the street cars and go to the St. James. But no street cars were in waiting and only one carriage.

"Go to the ——, lady?"

"No, I don't know that house," I replied; and giving my satchels in the ticket agent's care, I started out in the darkness, across the bridge, past dark streets and alleys, straight up Main street, past open saloons and billiard halls, but not a policeman in sight. So I kept an eye looking out on each side while I walked straight ahead with as firm and measured tread as though I commanded a regiment of soldiers, and I guess the clerk at the St. James thought I did, for he gave me an elegant suite of rooms with three beds. I gave two of them to my imaginary guards, and knelt at the other to thank the dear Father that He had brought me safely so near home.

"How much for my lodging?" I asked, in the morning.

"Seventy-five cents."

I almost choked as I repeated, "Seventy-five cents! Won't you please take fifty?"

"Why?"

"Because it is all the money I have, except a nickel."

"I suppose it will have to do," he said, and I jingled my fifty cents on the counter as loudly as though it was a whole dollar, but could not help laughing heartily at the low ebb of my finances. The several little extras I had met with had taken about all.

I then went to find brother Charlie's boarding-place and surprised him at the breakfast table.

August 1st, Charley and I visited Rock City, or rather, the city of rocks, just across the New York line. Houses of rock they are in size, but are only inhabited by sight-seers. I wish I could describe them to you, reader. All I know is, they are conglomerate rocks, made up of snowy white pebbles from the size of a pea to a hickory nut, that glisten in the sunlight, making the rocks a crystal palace. As I dig and try to dislodge the brightest from its bed of hardened sand, I wonder how God made the cement that holds them so firmly in place, and how and why He brought these rocks to the surface just here and nowhere else. Down, around, and under the rocks we climbed, getting lost in the great crevices, and trying to carve our names on the walls with the many that are chiseled there, but only succeeded in making "our mark." They are one of the beautiful, wonderful things that are beyond description.

Friday, August 3, I left on the Rochester & Pittsburgh R. R. for DuBois. Took a last look at Main street with its busy throng, and then out among the grand old hills that tower round with their forests of trees and derricks, winding round past Degoliar, Custer City, Howard Junction, and crossing east branch of "Tuna" creek. Everything is dumped down in wild confusion here—mountains and valleys, hills and hollows, houses and shanties, tanks and derricks, rocks and stones, trees, bushes, flowers, logs, stumps, brush, and little brooks fringed with bright bergamot flowers which cast their crimson over the waters and lade the air with their perfume. On we go past lots of stations, but there are not many houses after we get fairly out of the land of derricks. Through cuts and over tressels and fills—but now we are 17 miles from B., and going slowly over the great Kinzua bridge, which is the highest railway bridge in the world. It is 2,062 feet from abutment to abutment, and the height of rail above the bed of the creek is 302 feet. Kinzua creek is only a little stream that looks like a thread of silver in the great valley of hemlock forest. Will mother earth ever again produce such a grand forest for her children? Well, for once I feel quite high up in the world. Even Ex-President Grant, with all the honors that were heaped upon him while he "swung around the circle," never felt so elevated as he did when he came to see this bridge, and exclaimed while crossing it, "Judas Priest, how high up we are!"

It is well worth coming far to cross this bridge. I do not experience the fear I expected I would. The bridge is built wide, with foot walks at either side, and the cars run very slow.

One hotel and a couple of little houses are all that can be seen excepting trees. I do hope the woodman will spare this great valley—its noble trees untouched—and allow it to forever remain as one of Pennsylvania's grandest forest pictures.

Reader, I wish I could tell you of the great, broad, beautiful mountains of Pennsylvania that lift their rounded tops 2,000 to 2,500 feet above sea level. But as the plains of Nebraska are beyond description, so are the mountains.

J. R. Buchanan says: "No one can appreciate God until he has trod the plains and stood upon the mountain peaks."

To see and learn of these great natural features of our land but enlarges our love for the Great Creator, who alone could spread out the plains and rear the mountains, and enrich them with just what His children need. To wind around among and climb the broad, rugged mountains of Pennsylvania is to be constantly changing views of the most picturesque scenery of all the states of the Union.

Arrived at DuBois 5 P.M. This road has only been in use since in June, and the people gather round as though it was yet a novelty to see the trains come in. I manage to land safely with all my luggage in hand,

and make my way through the crowd to Dr. Smathers'. There stood Francis watching the darkies pass on their way to camp meeting; but when he recognized this darkey, he danced a jig around me, and ran on before to tell mamma "Auntie Pet" had come. I could not wait until I reached the "wee Margaretta" to call to her, and then came Sister Maggie, and were not we glad? and, oh! how thankful for all this mercy! and the new moon looked down upon us, and looked glad, too. These were glad, happy days, but I was not yet home. Father and Norval came in a few days. Norval to go with Charley to Nebraska, and father to take his daughter home.

"Well, Frank, you look just like the same girl after all your wandering," father said, as he wiped his eyes after the first greeting:

"Yes, nothing seems to change Pet, only she is much healthier looking than when she went away," Maggie said.

August 10. Father and I started early for a forty mile drive home, through farming and timber country. About one-third is cleared land, the rest is woods, stumps, and stones. At noon "Colonel" was fed, and we sat down under pine trees and took our lunch of dried buffalo meat from the west, peaches from the south, and apples from home. Well, I thought, that is just the way this world gets mixed up. It takes a mixture to make a good dinner, and a mixture to make a good world.

While going through Punxsutawney (Gnat-town). I read the sign over a shed, " Farming Implements." I looked, and saw one wagon, a plow, and something else, I guess it was a stump puller. I could not help comparing the great stock of farming implements seen in every little western town.

Along Big Mahoning creek, over good and bad roads, up hill and down we go, until we cross Little Mahoning—bless its bright waters!—and once more I look upon Smicksburg, my own native town—the snuggest, dearest little town I ever did see! and surrounded by the prettiest hills. If I was'nt so tired, I'd make a bow to every hill and everybody. Two miles farther on, up a long hill, and just as the sun sends its last rays aslant through the orchard, we halt at the gate of "Centre Plateau," and as I am much younger than father, I get out and swing wide the gate. It is good to hear the old gate creak a "welcome home" on its rusty hinges once more, and while father drives down the lane I slip through a hole in the fence, where the rails are crooked, and chase Rosy up from her snug fence corner; said "how do you do," to Goody and her calf, and start Prim into a trot; and didn't we all run across the meadow to the gate, where my dear mother stood waiting for me.

"Mother, dear, your daughter is safe home at last," I said, "and won't leave you soon again!"

Poor mother was too glad to say much. I skipped

along the path into the house, and Hattie (Charlie's wife) and I made such a fuss that we frightened Emma and Harry into a cry.

I carried the milk to the spring-house for mother, and while she strains it away, I tell her all about Uncle John's and the rest of the friends.

Come, reader, and sit down with me, and have a slice of my dear mother's bread and butter, and have some cream for your blackberries, and now let's eat. I've been hungry so long for a meal at home. And how good to go to my own little room, and thank God for this home coming at my own bedside, and then lay me down to sleep.

Then there were uncles, aunts, and cousins to visit and friends to see and tell all about my trip, and how I liked the West. Then "Colonel" was hitched up, and we children put off for a twenty mile ride to visit Brother Will's. First came Sister Lizzie to greet us, then dear May, shy little Frantie, and squealing, kicking Charlie boy was kissed—but where is Will?

"Out at the oats field?"

"Come, May, take me to your papa; I can't wait until supper time to see him." Together we climb the hill, then through the woods to the back field. Leaving May to pick huckleberries and fight the "skeeters," I go through the stubble. Stones are plenty, and I throw one at him. Down goes the cradle and up goes his hat, with "Three cheers for sister!"

As we trudge down the hill, I said: .

"Let's go West, Will, where you have no hills to climb, and can do your farming with so much less labor. Why, I didn't see a cradle nor a scythe while I was in Nebraska. Surely, it is the farmer's own state."

"Well, I would like to go if father and mother could go too, but I will endure the extra work here for the sake of being near them. If they could go along I would like to try life in the West."

Home again, and I must get to my writing, for I want to have my book out by the last of September. I had just got nicely interested, when mother puts her head in at the door, and says, with such a disappointed look:

"Oh! are you at your writing? I wanted you to help me pick some huckleberries for supper."

Now, who wouldn't go with a dear, good mother? The writing is put aside, and we go down the lane to the dear old woods, and the huckleberries are gathered.

Seated again——

"Frank," father says, "I guess you will have to be my chore boy while Norval is away. Come, I'd like you to turn the grindstone for me while I make a corn cutter."

Now, who wouldn't turn a grindstone for a dear, good father?

There stood father with a broken "sword of Bunker Hill" in his hand that he found on the battle field of Bunker Hill, in Virginia.

"Now, father, if you are sure that was a rebel sword, I'll willingly turn until it is all ground up; but if it is a Union sword, why then, "Hang the old sword in its place," and sharpen up your old corn cutters, and don't let's turn swords into plowshares now even though it be a time of peace."

I lock the door and again take up my pen. "Rattle, rattle at the latch," and "Oo witing, Aunt Pet? Baby and Emma wants to kiss Aunt Pet!" comes in baby voice through the key-hole. The key is quickly turned, and my little golden-haired "niece" and "lover" invade my sanctum sanctorum, and for a time I am a perfect martyr to kisses on the cheeks, mouth, and, as a last resort for an excuse, my little lover puts up his lips for a kiss "on oo nose." Now, who wouldn't be a martyr to kisses—I mean baby kisses?

Thus my time went until the grapes and peaches were ripe, and then came the apples—golden apples, rosy-cheeked apples, and the russet brown. And didn't we children help to eat, gather, store away, and dry until I finished the drying in a hurry by setting fire to the dry house. The cold days came before I got rightly settled down to write again, and although cold blows the wind and the snow is piling high, while the thermometer says 20° below, yet all I have to do is to take up a cracked slate and write. But I write right over the crack now until the slate is filled, and then it is copied off; I write I live the days all over again; eating Mrs. Skirving's good things, riding behind oxen and mules, crossing the Niobrara, viewing the Keya Paha, standing on Stone Butte, walking the streets of Valentine, and even yet I feel as though I was running the gauntlet, while the cowboys line the walks. Government mules are running off with me, now I am enjoying the ".Pilgrim's Retreat," and I go on until I have all told and every day lived over again in fond memory. And through it I learn a lesson of faith and trust.

So I wrote away until February 16, when I again left my dear home for the west, to have my book published. Went via DuBois and Bradford. Left Bradford March 19, for Buffalo, on the R. & P. R. R. The country along this road presents a wild picture, but I fear it would be a dreary winter scene were I to attempt to paint it, for snow drifts are yet piled high along the fence corners. At Buffalo I took the Michigan Central R. R. for Chicago. I catch a glimpse of Lake Erie as we leave Buffalo, and then we follow Niagara river north to the Falls. Reader, I will do the best I can to tell you of my car-window view of Niagara. We approach the Falls from the south, and cross the new suspension bridge, about two miles north of the Falls. Just below the bridge we see the whirlpool, where Capt. Webb, in his reckless daring, lost his life. The river here is only about 800 feet wide, but the water is over 200 feet deep. The banks of the river are almost perpendicular, and about 225 feet from top to the water's edge. Looking up the river, we can catch only a glimpse of the Falls, as the day is very dull, and it is snowing quite hard; but enough is seen to make it a grand picture. Across the bridge, and we are slowly rolling over the queen's soil. Directly south we go, following close to the river. When we are opposite the Falls the train is stopped for a few minutes, while we all look and look again. Had the weather been favorable, I would have been tempted to stop and see all that is to be seen. But I expect to return this way at a more favorable time, and shall not then pass this grand picture so quickly by. The spray rises high above the Falls, and if the day was clear, I am told a rainbow could be seen arching through the mist. The banks of the river above the Falls are low, and we can look over a broad sheet of blue water. But after it rushes over the Falls it is lost to our view. I wish I could tell you more, and tell it better, but no pen can do justice to Niagara Falls.

I was rather astonished at Canada. Why, I did not see more prairie or leveler land in the west than I did in passing through Canada. The soil is dark red clay, and the land low and swampy.

A little snow was to be seen along the way, but not as much as in New York; the country does not look very thrifty; poor houses and neglected farms; here and there are stretches of forest. Crossed the Detroit river on a boat as we did the Missouri, but it is dark and I can only see the reflection of the electric light on the water as we cross to the Michigan shore. The night is dark and I sleep all I can. I did not get to see much of Michigan as we reached Chicago at eight, Friday morning. But there was a friend there to meet me with whom I spent five days in seeing a little mite of the great city. Sunday, I attended some of the principal churches and was surprised at the quiet dress of the people generally and also to hear every one join in singing the good old tunes, and how nice it was; also a mission Sunday-school in one of the bad parts of the city, where children are gathered from hovels of vice and sin by a few earnest christian people who delight in gathering up the little ones while they are easily influenced. Well, I thought, Chicago is not all wicked and bad. It has its philanthropists and earnest christian workers, who are doing noble work. Monday, Lincoln Park was visited, and how I did enjoy its pleasant walks on that bright day, and throwing pebbles into Lake Michigan. Tuesday, went to see the panorama of the battle of Gettysburg. There now, don't ask me anything about it, only if you are in Chicago while it is on exhibition, go to corner Wabash avenue and Hubbard Court, pay your fifty cents and look for yourself. I was completely lost when I looked around, and felt that I had just woke up among the hills of Pennsylvania. But painted among the beautiful hills was one of the saddest sights eyes ever looked upon. The picture was life size and only needed the boom of the artillery and the groans of the dying to give it life. Wednesday morning brother Charles came with a party of twenty, bound for the Platte Valley, Nebraska, but I could not go with them as they went over the C. & N. W. R. R., and as I had been over that road, I wished to go over the C. B. & Q. R. R. for a change; so we met only to separate. I left on the 12.45, Wednesday, and for a way traveled over the same road that I have before described. There is not much to tell of prairie land in the early spring time and I am too tired to write. We crossed the Mississippi river at Burlington, 207 miles from Chicago, but it is night and we are deprived of seeing what would be an interesting view. Indeed it is little we see of Iowa, "beautiful land," as so much of it is passed over in the night. 482 miles from Chicago, we cross the Missouri river at Plattsmouth. 60 miles farther brings us to Lincoln, arriving there at 12 M. March 27. I surprised Deacon Keefer's again just at tea-time. Mother Keefer received me with open arms, and my welcome was most cordial from all, and I was invited to make my home with them during my stay in Lincoln.

My next work was to see about the printing of my book. I met Mr. Hathaway, of the State Journal

Co., and found their work and terms satisfactory, and on the morning of the 24th of April, just one year from the day our colony left Bradford and the work of writing my book began, I made an agreement with the Journal company for the printing of it. I truly felt that with all its pleasures, it had been a year of hard labor.

How often when I was busy plying the pen with all heart in the work, kind friends who wished me well would come to me with words of discouragement and ask me to lay aside my pen, saying:

"I do not see how you are to manage about its publication, and all the labor it involves."

"I do not know myself, but I have faith that if I do the work cheerfully, and to the best of my ability, and 'bearing well my burden in the heat of the day,' that the dear Lord who cared for me all through my wanderings while gathering material for this work, and put it into the hearts of so many to befriend me, will not forsake me at the last."

"Did He forsake me," do you ask?

"No, not for one moment." When asked for the name of some one in Lincoln as security, I went to one of my good friends who put their name down without hesitation.

"What security do you want of me?" I asked.

"Nothing, only do the best you can with your book."

"The dear Lord put it into your heart to do this in

answer to my many prayers that when the way was dark, and my task heavy, helping hands would be reached out to me."

"Why God bless you, little girl! The Lord will carry you through, so keep up brave heart, and do not be discouraged."

I would like to tell you the name of this good friend, but suffice it to say he is one whom, when but a lad, Abraham Lincoln took into his confidence, and by example taught him many a lesson of big-heartedness such as only Abraham Lincoln could teach.

Friday, May 9th. I went to Wymore to pay my last visit to my dear aunt, fearing that I would not find her there. But the dear Father spared her life and she was able to put her arms about me and welcome me with : "The Lord is very good to bring you to me in time. I was afraid you would come too late." Sunday her spirit went down to the water's edge and she saw the lights upon the other shore and said: "What a beautiful light! Oh! if I had my will I would cross over just now." But life lingered and I left her on Monday. Wednesday brought me this message: "Mother has just fallen asleep." With this shadow of sorrow upon me I went to Milford that day to begin my Maying of '84 with a row on the river and a sun-set view on the Blue.

"Is there a touch lacking or a color wanting?" I asked, as I looked up to the western sky at the beautiful picture, and down upon the mirror of waters, and saw its reflection in its depth.

The 15th of May dawned bright and beautiful; not a cloud flecked the sky all the livelong day. We gathered the violets so blue and the leaves so green of Shady Cliff and the Retreat, talking busily of other May-days, and thinking of the loved ones at home who were keeping my May-day in the old familiar places.

Then back to Lincoln carrying bright trophies of our Maying at Milford, and just at the close of day, when evening breathes her benediction, friends gathered round while two voices repeated: "With this ring I thee wed. By this token I promise to love and cherish."

And now reader, hoping that I may some day meet you in *my* "Diary of a Minister's Wife," I bid you Good-Bye.

www.ingramcontent.com/pod-product-compliance
Lightning Source LLC
Chambersburg PA
CBHW031947230426
43672CB00010B/2084